MENTAL HEAL.... ... ...R ALL

Community Well-being and the Church

Lorna H. Murray

British Library Cataloguing in Publication Data:
a catalogue record for this publication
is available from the British Library

ISBN   978-1-912052-59-2

Typeset in 11.5 pt Minion Pro at Haddington, Scotland

Printing and cover design by
T J Books Limited, Padstow

Covid-19 is destroying lives and devastating communities across the world, and the lockdowns put in place to try to control its rapid spread are adding to our distress. The requirements of lockdown rules and social distancing measures are having a hugely negative impact on the well-being of so many of us._

This virus has brought with it not only illness but fear: fear of the illness itself and fear of others. We are becoming afraid of contact with other people – with people who may be carrying the virus with them into our country, our neighbourhood, our home. Covid-19 is having an impact on our mental health, as people throughout the world experience the intense loneliness caused by 'self-isolation' and 'social distancing'. So many of us are missing the daily informal contacts we are used to with family, friends and neighbours.

The poorest people, and those who were already the most vulnerable among us, are those whose lives have been hardest hit. Daily wage earners and those working in seasonal or low-paid jobs are having to choose between hunger for themselves and their families, or continuing to work and thereby risking both catching and spreading the virus. Millions across the world have no access to the water essential for hygiene and the frequent washing of hands.

In our lifetime, nothing has revealed so clearly the inter-connection of human societies, nor of the tragic effects of prioritising economic growth over human well-being and the rights of the individual over respect for others and responsibility for all.

The economics of trade and the movement of goods across national and international boundaries encouraged the rapid spread of the virus. Before the risk was fully recognised, covid-19 was being carried by executive and leisure travellers. And now, even with the knowledge we have about the ease and rapidity with which the virus can spread, there remains pressure to 'open up the economy' and to 'get back to normal'.

Our inter-connectedness has become a threat. Yet it is through our connecting with each other – in our relationships with family and friend, with neighbour and stranger – that we find meaning and purpose to life and discover how to live well. We must re-discover the benefits *of connection and challenge the systems that abuse and cause such harm.*

Signs of such re-discovery have already been seen in the support given in local communities to those asked to shield in their home during lockdown, and in the many thoughtful and caring actions of so many. Phone calls to neighbours known to be struggling with loneliness, adding a small surprise treat to shopping left on a doorstep, chatting with strangers on our daily walks and so much more. Even as we have appreciated the contacts made possible via the internet, we have been missing and longing for personal contact and human touch.

Humans are relational beings. People need people: God made us that way. We are created to be inter-dependent. Rather than planning a return to 'how things were', and continuing with system that prioritise profits over people, making the livelihoods of millions in countries across the world dependent on the finance and trade deals of the rich and powerful, it is time to seek a 'new normal' in which the well-being of individuals and of communities becomes the 'new priority' for governments throughout the world.

I had been working on this book long before the words 'coronavirus', 'lockdown' or 'social distancing' entered our vocabulary. The stories and reflections contained within it are intended to help church members to identify ways of encouraging and enabling mental health and well-being. They focus on the importance of church involvement in local partnerships aiming to create communities of well-being. Its contents are now more important than ever.

Our Saviour, Jesus Christ, teaches us the value of all life and demonstrates in his own life how we are to respect, care for and care about each and every person as a loved and cherished child of God. As followers of His teaching and example, members of the church have much to contribute to encouraging the caring, sharing and mutually supportive relationships that that enable us all to live well. Our commitment is to obey the command of God to love and serve Him through our loving and serving of our neighbour – whoever and wherever that neighbour might be (St. Luke 10.27-28).

The church worldwide is a network of disciples of Jesus. Becoming a member of this network identifies us as such disciples and makes clear our commitment to a life of seeking justice and showing love, as we live in humble fellowship with our God (Micah 6.8). Just as the word 'church' was never intended only as a definition of the buildings in which Christians gather, so 'becoming a church member' was never intended to be primarily about signing up to the doctrines of a specific denomination or having the right to a vote within its structures and organisation.

Lockdown has reminded us that 'church' is 'people' and that membership is about the outworking of our faith as we care for and about everyone in the communities in which we live. Church is about relationships and about celebrating our inter-dependence. We are dependent on God for life itself. Our God has created us as beings who need each another, and who seek out the company of others for support and for friendship.

As in the saying that the flutter of a butterfly's wings on one continent begins the breeze that sways the ripening grain on another, so do our actions affect the well-being of our neighbours, whether next door or on the far side of the world.

Covid-19 has highlighted this reality in the devastation it continues to cause.

The good news, however, is that our words and our actions – when we choose the way of love and compassion, of caring and sharing – can enable the well-being of all people. Our God has created us to be inter-dependent: it is in caring and supportive relationships with each other that well-being is found.

As disciples of Jesus, our commitment is to follow faithfully the way of living that He has shown us: trust in God and love of people. And so we work in our communities to renew hope, to love and to care, to encourage well-being; seeking for all people the 'life in all its fullness' (John 10.10) that is God's promise to the world.

This book has been written from Lorna's experience of a life lived in the service of others as a person of faith; but her warmth and compassion for her fellow human beings makes this a collection of stories and reflections relevant to anyone trying to understand what it means to achieve mental wellbeing in this challenging world.

I was drawn into the stories about people's lives and experiences that I could identify with and found myself being led through the reflections on individual and community resilience in a way that challenged me to think, but left me feeling positive and uplifted and more aware of my own beliefs.

Lorna's open, accessible story-telling style explores all the big questions such as prejudice, acceptance, inclusion and hope with gentle ease, and for me was the most succinct and meaningful discussion of the necessary inter-dependence of community and individual wellbeing that I have read.

Frances Simpson, Chief Executive, Support in Mind Scotland

With the coming of Covid, we all have begun to think more about mental health issues. Many of us have begun to understand in new ways the devastating effects of loneliness, the frustration of being housebound, the fear and anxiety of changes in our work life, or worse, the ending of our work life. Very quickly we have discovered that we are not really individuals; we are deeply interconnected. We need one another for the health of our bodies, minds and spirits. In this book Lorna Murray gives us some wonderful guidance as to how we can make this revelation of our interdependence an opportunity to create communities within which mental health is a healing priority. Through stories and reflections she opens up new understandings and fresh perspectives on health, wellness, friendship and community. This is definitely a book for the times. Reading it is a blessing.

*Revd Professor John Swinton, Professor in Practical Theology
and Pastoral Care, University of Aberdeen*

Contents

Prologue

Swifts. Dozens of them. Darting in and out among the branches of the trees. Not where I usually see them, swooping low over the River Don near my home in Aberdeenshire, but here, in the south-eastern region of Nigeria. I have just arrived in the village that is to be my home for the next few weeks, and am watching these birds, as I sit outside, talking with my new friends, in the cool of the evening breeze.

The birds may be familiar, but everything else is new to me. It is hard to believe that I really *am* in Africa - that I really *have* been given this wonderful opportunity to come here to learn about mental health care in this village where people struggling to cope with their difficulties are welcomed, supported and cared for until they are well enough to return to their families. I ask the group of women I am sitting with, 'Are these birds up there in the trees swifts?' 'Yes,' I am told. 'These are our swifts. They come in this season every year'. Another woman adds, 'We were told that they fly to where you come from to build their nests and raise their young.'

'They're our swifts', these women tell me. Yet, back home, we think of them as *ours*. Because they return year after year, we call them *our* birds: 'we say that they fly south to visit you', I comment. 'And *we* say that *our* birds go to visit *you*', is the smiling reply.

This is a moment of bonding for us, as we relax in the evening sunshine and gaze up at the swifts flying high above us. These birds, happy to make their home among us both, remind us of our shared humanity. I am Scottish. These women are Igbo. Our cultures are so different, and there are moments when it is hard for us to understand each other. In the weeks that lie ahead I will learn much from my new friends, as they teach me new skills and as we tell stories of our very different experiences.

What we have in common, however, is more significant than anything that might divide us. We are all loved by God. With God's help, we can not only learn from each other; we can discover how to love one another.

Introduction

Looking back over almost twenty years' work as a Mental Health Chaplain, within the NHS in Scotland and in England, I am aware of how much my faith has encouraged me and enabled me to work effectively.

Spending time in Bible study gave me a clearer understanding of how to help people who are struggling to cope with pain or distress. Reading our scriptures highlighted for me the importance of social action and working for justice in enabling mental health and well-being. Reflection on my relationship with God, and on my own need for love and care, helped me to listen more sensitively to the needs of others. Prayer brought new insights into how to care for people who are feeling that life is no longer worth living. And throughout my own times of depression, the friendship of colleagues was there as a reminder that the love of God is with us always, even in the darkest of places.

Almost every day, I met with people who were struggling to cope *alone*. Some told me of how their family had abandoned them; others of the abuse they had to endure daily from neighbours. They spoke of the prejudice they faced from work colleagues and of being excluded from social activities. People living with mental health problems, whether short bouts of anxiety or depression, or the more long-term effects of such illnesses as schizophrenia or bi-polar disorder, frequently told me that it was the prejudice of others, rather than the symptoms of their illness, that made life so hard for them.

Commitment to following the teaching and example of Jesus requires us to challenge such prejudice. Our faith tells us that we are all made in the image of our Creator God, and that God loves and cares for each and every person. The waters of the river of justice we read of in the book of the prophet Amos (Amos 5.24) are to bring new life and new hope to every community.

This book is about mental health and well-being. It looks at how our faith can encourage us and guide us, as we help one another live mentally healthy lives and journey towards the fullness of life that is God's promise for us all. The purpose of the book is to encourage us, as Christians, to be more aware of how to support people going through a time of poor mental health, and those living with a diagnosed mental illness. Understanding their needs, and working together with them and with others in our communities, we in the church can become more involved in the creation of communities of well-being.

Improving the mental health and well-being of individuals and of communities is a priority in Scotland: several initiatives are being promoted by the Scottish Government and developed by a range of statutory and voluntary organisations. The church has a significant contribution to make. At national and at local level, the church can enter into partnerships with organisations involved in developing the well-being of individuals and of communities. Locally, congregations have many opportunities for working together with others to improve the care and support available, while also continuing to ensure that its pastoral presence is available and accessible to all.

As Christians, we are people committed by our faith to loving our neighbour, and to doing all we can to encourage well-being. Wherever welcome and acceptance is experienced, our mental health has the opportunity to flourish. Caring relationships can keep hope alive through the times of darkness that threaten our well-being. Companionship and support can prevent stresses and strains or everyday worries from becoming feelings of anxiety or despair.

In this book, we focus on three main aspects of our Christian commitment to well-being. We look at caring *about* each other, as we seek to ensure that the communities we live in are places where everyone is accepted, and where all are enabled to live in peace, and with adequate resources. We reflect on what it means to care *for* each other, as we support one another through the painful and difficult times that affect us all. And we consider, too, how we can share the insights of our faith, as we work together for the well-being of our local communities. Each aspect is equally important. All three are essential to Christian pastoral care. The prophet Micah reminds us of them when he tells us what God expects, and requires, of his people: we are to 'do what is just, to show constant love, and to live in humble fellowship with our God'.

The stories at the beginning of each chapter, and the reflections that follow them, emphasise these dimensions of Christian care. Early chapters focus on our inter-dependence, and stress the importance of welcoming and accepting people just as they are. Next, the focus is on the journey towards well-being and we think, in particular, how to enable each other to live well, even if going through a period of mental illness. We then consider the potential value of sharing stories from the Bible, and look at the problems – as well as the benefits – of talking about our relationship with God.

Many of the stories told are of people I met during my years spent working as a Mental Health Chaplain. All the stories are true, although some details, and all names, have been changed, to ensure confidentiality. I have chosen to share these particular stories, so as to highlight some of the issues and difficulties that we may encounter as we seek to help one another. In the reflections that follow each story, questions are asked: questions about our faith and our practice. How can we help and encourage *this particular individual* through *this particular difficulty*? How is *this particular interpretation* of scripture influencing the way we care?

When reading each of the chapters in this book, I invite you to reflect on the ways in which your faith influences the way that you care. I encourage you to think about your own experience of life, and about the situations of the people around you, and to take a fresh look at familiar passages from the Bible. By thinking in this reflective way – in time spent with our own thoughts, in discussion with friends or colleagues, in Bible Study, and in prayer – we can begin to identify ways of caring that encourage the well-being of us all.

You are invited to read, reflect on, and discuss the stories that begin each chapter. Think about the issues that, over the years, these people have shared with me. Talk about the feelings these experiences aroused in them as they struggled to cope. Share the emotions you yourself feel as you read their stories.

Use the stories and the reflections as discussion-starters when considering what is needed in your own community. Be challenged to think of new – and better – ways to help the people you know and care about. Develop ideas about what would work best in your own situation. Plan what would be most effective in your own community. Then work together to make your local area into a community of well-being; a place in which *everyone* is enabled, and encouraged, to *live well*.

Chapter One

Swimming Pigeons

Story

Walking around the pond near where I used to live in Edinburgh, I watched a young boy feeding the ducks, while pigeons gathered expectantly close by. The boy was asking the adult with him if pigeons could swim. 'No', she replied. 'Oh,' said the boy, adding, 'But ducks can'. 'That's right', said the woman, 'ducks can swim, but pigeons can't'. 'Why?' asked the boy. 'Well,' continued the woman, 'pigeons are a different sort of bird: they fly, but they can't swim'. The inevitable 'why?' was asked again. 'Because they can't', was the rather frustrated response. Undaunted, the boy – perhaps aware that he himself was expected to 'do his best' or 'try harder' – continued to question: 'but if the pigeons tried *really hard*, don't you think they could learn?'

Reflection

Some abilities come naturally. We may think of them as talents we are fortunate to have been born with, or we might believe them to be special gifts from God.

Much of what we, as human beings, are capable of doing – however we view such abilities – has to be learned. It takes time to develop most skills, and many we can improve only by much practice. Some of us take to the complexities of mathematics like the proverbial 'ducks to water', while others, like myself, settle down to learn our 'times tables' by rote. Some of us have an instinct for rhythm, and can dance to the beat while still at nursery school, while others of us learn to accept our 'two left feet'.

For all of us, however, there are some abilities that we just don't have, and we must learn to live within our limitations. Discovering that we feel dizzy and sick looking down from a great height might only be a minor inconvenience, leading us to choose white-water rafting rather than mountain climbing as a hobby. It could, however, cause us severe anxiety when we find out that our new employer's workplace is on the top storey of a new office block. During our school years, we may be happy to realise that our test results show we have clearly not been born with the brains to become a rocket scientist, and content to focus our attention on less academic subjects. But if, as a result, our parents show disappointment, we may grow up with a sense of failure. Were they to turn up at our school, demanding we take the subjects they believe are more important, we might find ourselves stressed or depressed, or made fun of by our class-mates.

What we are unable to do can make life hard for each of us: it is, however, part of what it means to be human. Life is harder than it need be when we are expected to cope on our own, or where asking for help is considered a sign of weakness. *That*, though, is *not* part of being human: *inter*-dependence, not *in*dependence, is a characteristic of human life.

In my work as a Mental Health Chaplain, trying to encourage the people who come to me for support, I always reassured them that asking for help is not a sign of weakness: it is, rather, a sign of healthy self-awareness. Recognising when we need help is an acknowledgement of our inter-dependence. It is one of the first steps we can take in improving our situation, or coping with the difficulties we currently face, as we learn to appreciate and to celebrate our shared humanity.

The realisation that there are some things we are unable to do is rarely a problem in itself: it is one of the realities of life. Most young children are happy to call out for the help they need: 'I can't reach' and 'help me' are words common in most households. What children cannot do by themselves only becomes a problem when others expect something different. 'When I was your age, I could tie my own shoelaces' can discourage the child who struggles with manual dexterity. And 'if you can't reach, you can't have' – where it does not lead to hazardous attempts at indoor mountaineering – may dent the confidence of the timid child.

Inability not *disability*

Many of the difficulties we face, in relation to the things we cannot do for, or by, ourselves, become problems mainly because of the unfair expectations of others, or the prejudice of those who define some – but only some – of our human *in*abilities as *dis*abilities.

'If I can do it, so can you,' can, in the right context and with the right attitude, be an encouragement; often, however, it is said as a claim to superiority. 'If I can do it, then so should you (but you can't do it, because you are not as able as I am)' is the message that is heard, and also often intended. 'If I can do it, then so can – or should – you' also so often indicates a refusal to help. When help is refused, and inter-dependence denied, then the *in*ability we may be leaning to cope with can become a *dis*ability that is hard to live with.

The 'if you can't reach, you can't have' attitude is so common in our society that we often scarcely notice it, unless we are directly affected by it. 'What makes you think you could be a nurse, when you sometimes get depressed?' 'It's not possible for you to share in leading our worship – you can't even read'. Such comments may not often be *said*; but they *are* often implied.

Where we fail to accept the abilities *and* inabilities that we all have, and refuse to acknowledge that *inter*-dependence – not *in*dependence – is a key characteristic of being human, then prejudice will continue and people will go on feeling rejected or unwelcome. The *dis*abilities that some of us 'have' are, in fact, often 'given to' us by the prejudices of others. Along with the label 'disabled' come exclusion and lack of acceptance. The implication is that those of us whom others have identified as 'disabled' are somehow not as fully human as the ones who have labelled us.

As a child, in the early nineteen-sixties, I was taken on holiday one summer to the north of Scotland. I went with my elder sister, who had been born with what, in those days, was called 'severe mental and physical handicaps'. Nearing lunch time one day, we stopped outside a remote café, and I was told to go in and ask if there was a table for us, and to check whether the entrance was wide enough for my sister's wheelchair. A table was, indeed, available, and I worked out that if both of the doors to the café could be opened, and not just the side that was currently unbolted, then there was plenty room for the wheelchair to go through. The owner watched me carefully studying the door, and came across to ask what I was doing. When I explained, he said he was sorry, but we could not, after all, come in. At least, the rest of the family could come in, and he would, if we would like it, bring some food out to the car for my sister. When I asked why he was saying this, he replied that he did not want my sister in the café, in case seeing her there put other diners off their meal. Needless to say, we did without lunch that day.

There is general agreement that 'things have improved since then'; but any experience of prejudice or exclusion is one experience too many. Only recently I spoke to a Community Psychiatric Nurse who had spent a long weekend in a 'Bed & Breakfast' with some members of the mental health drop-in club where she works. They had received a warm welcome and had enjoyed a wonderful weekend – until they arrived back there on their last evening. They were met by the landlady, who asked if they would mind having breakfast an hour earlier the following morning. They were happy to oblige until one of them, out of polite interest, asked the reason for the change. They were horrified at the response. A new group was travelling overnight, arriving in time for breakfast, and she did not think they would like it if they knew that the beds they would sleep in that night had been used by people who had a mental illness. The landlady had noticed that their bill had been paid by a mental health care organisation: though she was happy to accept their money, she was not prepared to accept *them*. They agreed to the earlier mealtime, rather than make the complaint that would no doubt convince the landlady that they were all as 'mad' as she clearly thought they might be. But they vowed never to return.

'Success' or support?

It is strange how, so often, it is the people who have plenty – money, opportunities, influence – who claim that their needs are more important than the needs of everyone else.

These 'successful', and often powerful, people seem unable, or unwilling, to recognise the damage that their attitude is doing, to themselves as well as to others. At the same time as they talk proudly of their independence and their ability to 'succeed' on their own, they claim to have needs that must take priority over the needs of others who may be struggling to cope. Such lack of self-awareness is unhealthy: failure to acknowledge their need of others results in a lack of personal mental health and well-being.

Because they deny, or choose to ignore, the contribution that their own power and 'success' is adding to the difficulties of others, their lack of acknowledgement of human inter-dependence also puts at risk the mental health and well-being of those around them.

This imbalance of power is as damaging at national and international level as it is where it exists within local communities. Evidence of the damage caused is seen almost daily on our television screens. We hear news of famine, or flood, or epidemic in countries struggling to feed and educate their people while also repaying the 'loans with strings attached' that their leaders have been forced to take from the governments of the 'rich west'.

This book is not about international relations. But it does consider an issue that is of *world-wide* concern. All over the world are people whose reluctance to acknowledge our inter-dependence – with each other and with the whole of creation – is hindering the development of community well-being. All over the world there are individuals, and groups, who are 'disabled' by the selfishness and greed of others. In almost every community, there will be someone whose life is being made miserable by the stigma and prejudice of others.

We need only reflect on issues of current concern to see the extent to which the prejudice of others adds to the problems of so many people in the world today. Think of people who live not only with the diagnosis of AIDS, or of schizophrenia, and the effects of these illnesses, but who also must cope with the added difficulties created by stigma and prejudice. Think of all those in poorer communities whose experience of life is restricted, because their family cannot afford to buy wheelchair or walking aid, or purchase the medication that would ease the symptoms of their illness. Compare the amount of money made at a fund-raising event in aid of a cancer care charity with that received at a similar event to raise money to fund a drop-in centre for people who have a mental illness. Cancer and depression are both illnesses, and, while it is true that those who live with each of these conditions may find themselves pitied or perceived as 'different', those with depression, or any other form of mental illness, are much more likely to be avoided and excluded from community life.

Inter-dependent living

We need the swifts referred in the *Prologue*. Just as we need *all* of creation. And all of creation needs us. Inter-dependence. Birds need trees; trees need insects; insects need flowers; flowers need water. The list goes on. And on. We need the natural world: and it needs us. To care for, and be cared for by, all that lives and grows within it.

As human beings, we are inter-dependent, not only with nature, but also with one another. We are not only inter-dependent with family and friends and in our local community, but inter-dependent with people all over the world. We all need each other. And we all need to care; both to *give* care and to *receive* it.

The chapters of this book encourage us to celebrate our human inter-dependence. Through our inter-dependence, we can discover well-being: for ourselves, for our local community and for all our neighbours, far and near. The more we learn to enjoy and to celebrate our inter-dependence, the more we will discover how sharing and caring can create the kind of community in which everyone is enabled to 'fly free'.

The aim of this book is to encourage the creation of communities of well-being in which each and every one of us is valued and accepted, not only for what we can *do*, but – primarily – because we *are there*. It is our *being* that gives us value: God loves all that he creates and asks of us that we love one another – just as *we are*.

Pastoral care and well-being

Throughout the rest of this book, the focus is on our well-being in relation to *mental health*. We consider the specific needs we might have when going through a period of living with mental illness. We reflect on the significance of mental health to our well-being as individuals and as communities.

The presence of caring friends, and supportive relationships, encourages in us all a sense of well-being. Feeling safe and secure, having a warm and comfortable home, and pleasant surroundings to relax in all contribute to our well-being. Freedom from pain, too, is important if we are to live well. Living a mentally healthy life, however, is not dependent upon being free from illness of any kind, including mental illness.

Pain and suffering do, of course, have a negative effect on our mental health. We all know how hard it can be to feel good about ourselves or take an interest in anything when we are in pain. This is true regardless of whether our pain is caused by heart disease or the despairing darkness of depression. But, just as with physical illness, with appropriate treatment, care and support, we can both *feel* well and *live* well.

We can feel good when the circumstances we live in are pleasant and when we feel that our life has meaning and purpose. Enjoyable and positive relationships, and having people around us to share in the ups and downs of life with, can make many problems bearable. Feeling ourselves accepted by others contributes greatly to our mental health and well-being.

The pastoral care that is the subject of this book – as it focuses on mental health and well-being – is both pro-active and re-active. Our Christian responsibility is to care. We care *about* each other, as we do what we can to ensure that our community is a good place to live in, and we care *for* each other, as support is offered in difficult times.

The responsibility to react in times of need is highlighted by Jesus in his Parable of the Good Samaritan (St. Luke 10. 25-37). By telling us this story, Jesus is teaching us that love of neighbour goes beyond caring for our friends and for the people we like. Loving our neighbour extends to caring for the stranger, for those with whom we feel we have nothing in common and for people we dislike or who may dislike us. What this parable does not mention, however, but which is just as much a part of the love of neighbour that we are called to, is the pro-active caring about each other that enables us all to live well.

Pro-active pastoral care involves the search for justice, as we do all that is possible to prevent problems and difficult situations arising. Pro-active pastoral care challenges us to find ways of ensuring the safety of people who travel on the road from Jerusalem to Jericho. If robbers attack because they are desperate to feed their starving children, then ways must be found to share resources more fairly, so that everyone has enough. If street lights, or police patrols, are only provided on the urban highways but not on the rural byways, then we may need to challenge the priorities of our government, to ensure that all can travel safely.

The prophet Micah emphasises these pro-active and re-active dimensions of care. Our lives, he tells us, are to be rooted in our faith and our trust in God, enabling us to 'do what is just [and] show constant love' (Micah 6.8). But we can only do that if we walk humbly with our God. We listen for God's guidance and we ask for God's help.

Mental health

Is this book on caring about each other's mental health and the well-being of our communities saying anything different from any other book about pastoral care? The answer is – both yes and no. For the church to be involved in mental health care is, in many ways, no different from the work we are already doing in our pastoral care. Alastair Campbell, who for many years taught the subjects of pastoral care and theology at Edinburgh University, defined pastoral care as:

> that aspect of the ministry of the Church which is concerned with the well-being of individuals and of communities.[1]

Understood in this way, we can say that this book is, indeed, a book about pastoral care.

But it is different in that it is a book about pastoral care with a specific focus on creating mentally healthy communities. Mental health is essential to our well-being: our well-being as individuals and as communities. The World Health Organisation[2] reminds us that 'there can be no health without mental health'. To experience well-being, we must take care of our mental health.

Mental health care is not something we 'give to' other people: it is a way of life. Discovering more about how to look after our own mental health is a significant part of our journey to fullness of life. Enabling ourselves, and those around us, to experience such mental health is, therefore, an important aspect of Christian commitment. Working to make the communities we live in into places where everyone is valued and where love is shared and hope renewed is also part of this responsibility to care. We are co-workers

---

1   Campbell, Alastair V., ed., *A dictionary of pastoral care*, London: SPCK, 1987, p. 188.

2   https://www.who.int/news-room/fact-sheets/detail/mental-health-strengthening-our-response (accessed 14 August 2020).

with Christ as we live to make God's Kingdom a reality 'on earth as it is in heaven'.

The other way this book is different is because, as a necessary part of its focus on mental health and well-being, it also aims to help us to offer appropriate pastoral care to people going through a period of mental illness.

The church in recent times has not been good at this. Like the majority of the population, Christians have thought of people who have a mental illness as being 'different', or as people to be avoided, or even feared. Victorian society built asylums and intended them to offer sanctuary; to be safe places for treatment and rehabilitation. But these asylums were built 'round the bend'. They were out of sight of the local community. And being out of sight soon meant that the people residing there were ignored or forgotten about. These places often now lie empty. Attitudes are beginning to change. But such change is slow and is far from widespread. People living with a range of mental health problems still have to cope with prejudice.

It is often with the best of intentions, however, that our churches today are reluctant to become involved in caring for people experiencing mental distress. 'I was worried that I might upset her', or 'I thought it was better that he talked about that with his doctor', are examples of comments that I heard frequently when, working as a Mental Health Chaplain, I led discussions in church meetings. But how many of us avoid asking a friend how their operation has gone, or a neighbour recovering from surgery if they need help with meals or shopping? Offering to help at times of illness and visiting the sick at home or in hospital are seen as priorities of pastoral care: why should this be any different when the illness is illness of the mind?

It is, of course, important that people having serious problems with their mental health visit their doctor, so that appropriate medical or therapeutic care can be given. Just as damaging as avoiding or ignoring people with mental illness is the refusal of some Christian groups to accept that the distress being experienced is, indeed, illness. Telling people that their mental distress is a sign that they lack faith, or insisting that prayer, not medication, will restore to health, does more harm than good.

Each of these attitudes towards mental illness, held by some Christian individuals and groups, risks adding to any worry or distress already being experienced due to the symptoms of illness. Those of us who develop a mental illness – just like those who develop a physical illness – need care and prayer, comfort and practical support as well as medicine and therapy. The church can do much, in practical ways, to help people through a time of mental illness. And during such times our concern, acceptance and love can give strength to cope and hope to sustain.

Community well-being

I hope that the contents of this book may be helpful to anyone seeking to improve the well-being of their local community.

It is, however, written especially for those of us whose commitment to care is motivated by Christian faith and by the teaching of Jesus. It is he who teaches us that it is our responsibility – as his disciples – to ensure that everyone can experience the love of God. This love is made real in the relationships we share, in the acceptance we are given, and in the acknowledgement of our value and worth that we receive, not because of what we can achieve, but simply because we *are*.

As we work to create communities in which all are welcome, all are cared for, and all are valued and respected for the unique contribution that each has to offer – just by *being there* – each renewed community can become a place where mental health and well-being flourish. Such communities can also become signs of hope: hope to others in our world that, even in the midst of pain and distress, new life can be found.

Pigeons cannot swim. And neither should they. For each part of creation has its own unique purpose: ducks swim, pigeons fly. As humans, each of us is a unique individual, bringing our own unique contribution within inter-dependent community living. Where the community in which we live recognises this, and values each and every one of its_members, then all of us are enriched, encouraged and enabled. Such inter-dependence and acceptance enable the development of communities of well-being, in which the community as a whole can both swim and fly as it lives to bring new life and new hope to *all* who live within it.

Chapter Two

I Need my Dog

Story

I am about six years old, and each Sunday I am taken to church. After a hymn, a prayer and a talk to us children, I file out of the worship area and into the hall where the primary department of the Sunday School meets.

One Sunday, we listen to the story of how a man described as 'paralysed' is healed by Jesus after the man's friends lower him through the roof of the house in which Jesus is teaching a crowd of people. It is a story we find hard to believe. 'How', asks one young voice, 'how could they get him up onto the roof?' Another hand goes up, and 'how could he carry his bed home all by himself?' is asked. So we are told about houses in those days being different to ours: they had outside staircases and flat roofs. And there is an explanation about the bed, too: beds in those days, we are told, were more like what we know as sleeping bags, so the man could easily roll it up and carry it home. The story is not so difficult to understand after all: we can accept it as one that really happened, and not as a fairy story in which things can happen by magic.

But what of the man who was now able to walk? How did *that* happen? We do not ask. Jesus, according to this and other Bible stories, was a teacher, and, as teacher, he has told the man to do something, so he does it. What else would we expect? By six years old we have already discovered the consequences of disobeying the teacher. The details of the conversation Jesus has with the crowd holds little interest for us: we are all well-used to finding more interesting things to think about when the adults around us start talking among themselves.

But the story is worrying me. I keep asking myself the question: 'how is it that the man was able to walk?' Something inside me, however, tells me that is not a question to be asked. And I don't have the words to describe my feelings, so I keep them to myself.

Once at home, though, I need to think. As always, Kimmy the dog is at the door, tail wagging, ready to welcome me home. I retreat upstairs to my bedroom, and he pads faithfully up behind me. We curl up on the rug, to work this out together. 'Jesus told that man to get up and walk', I explain to my dog, 'and he did. But *how*? If he's never been able to walk before, how can he do it now?' I think about the story and try to remember the words we had listened to at Sunday School. I'd heard about faith, of course; knew it was something that people who go to church are expected to 'have'. I had also heard about God, and how God gave us Jesus to love us and look after us. 'The man must have asked Jesus to make him able to walk', I decide. And a lick from Kimmy convinces me I am right.

That, however, is not the end of my worry. I have a sister, three years older than me, who has never been able to walk. So, I think to myself, if she could ask Jesus to let her walk, then she could do it too, just like the man in the story. That is my problem. I am sure that she cannot ask for herself. She can only manage to say a few words, and in my six-year-old way I am aware of how little she can understand: the connection between the words she says and their meaning is often just not there. She just says them, as though she enjoys the sounds they make. So how can she ask Jesus to let her walk? 'She can't', is what I decide. And if she can't, then I must do it for her.

We go back downstairs, my faithful four-legged friend and I, and into the sitting room. I wait. Teatime will come, and we will be left alone while the meal is prepared. Soon, with just the three of us there, I put my plan into action. I go to my sister in her wheelchair. I unbuckle the straps that are holding her body upright, and say out loud: 'Jesus, help her to stand up and walk'.

She shudders and falls. Bang! Onto the floor. And the adults come running. 'What have you done?' they shout at me. 'You stupid girl! Why did you undo her straps? You *know* she can't sit up on her own'. I stay quiet: I cannot tell them what really happened. I accept my punishment, and return upstairs, relieved that, as always, the dog takes my side in any argument, and follows me back to my bedroom.

I am devastated. What has gone wrong? I've asked Jesus for help, but no help has come. What is wrong with me? Whatever this faith-thing is – I know I haven't got it.

Reflection

This story raises many questions: questions about how the accounts of healing by Jesus can be understood and interpreted, as well as questions about relationships between those of us who require particular forms of help and those who are able to offer it. Although this story is not specifically about mental health, it *is* about well-being. Reflecting on it will, it is hoped, help us to focus on the main concern of this chapter: how to identify appropriate ways of caring for, and about, the people around us in our own communities.

Caring for others and seeking the well-being of everyone in the community around us requires us to give careful thought about what the Bible says to us about healing and wholeness, and about how we understand the stories told of Jesus healing sickness and disease. We will look at this later in this chapter, and again in the chapter entitled '*What's a yoke, then?*'. Here, however, we focus on the story above, and the questions it raises about our perception of what it means to care.

Reflection needs to be rooted in our experience; so, as we consider the various issues raised by this story, we keep returning to questions related to real life experience. 'How might each character in the story have been feeling?' 'What would I have felt in the same situation?' 'What would I have done?' 'What might have been more helpful?'

Questions such as these are important to keep in mind as we reflect on each situation we face. They help us to see how the same experience can affect different people in different ways. They remind us that the time and the place in which an event occurs influence the effect it has on us, as well as vary the responses we may make. What we do, and how we feel, are influenced by who we are, the culture we live in and what we ourselves have experienced. Becoming more aware of ourselves at any given moment in our life helps us to reflect more effectively.

Who we are – our basic personality – affects the way we learn, as well as how our attitudes and our understandings are formed. These change throughout time, as we grow and develop, and as our circumstances alter. Such changes, in turn, have an impact on our attitudes and understandings. Reflection is a life-long process.

What also changes, however, are assumptions about what is good practice in terms of caring for others. What is possible and acceptable in a small rural community may not be appropriate in the context of city life. Ideas that were hailed as 'models for best practice' in one era are frowned upon in another. Cultural differences also abound. The care needs of the Igbo villagers referred to in the Prologue will be significantly different from those of men and women living in isolated rural areas of Scotland.

Taking time to listen to the stories of individuals and communities is a vital first step in developing appropriate community care for mental health and well-being. In addition, however, it is also necessary to learn from theories of care, whether rooted in the understandings of health and social care practice or in the teachings of our faith community and our experience of God.

Reflection that considers what is appropriate and helpful from *all* these perspectives is reflection likely to lead us towards improved community care. Such reflection can enable church congregations to be useful and active partners in the creating of communities of well-being, in which the inter-dependence of us all is not only recognised but also celebrated, and in which each one of us feels welcomed and accepted for who we are.

Caring is good: but for whose benefit?

What is of crucial importance in this story is its reminder that caring is good: the desire to help someone else is to be encouraged and developed. As a young child, hearing a Bible story about Jesus healing, my intention was to help my sister to be able to walk. Even an acknowledgement that, within that desire to help may have been a longing for a playmate who could join in more with the activities I enjoyed, does not deny the good inherent in the wish to 'make better'.

At a simple and straightforward level, the majority of us are well-intentioned towards other people. We consider it 'natural' when we see a mother or father pick up their crying child, ask the child where it hurts and then kiss that knee or elbow to 'make it better'. We describe a friend, or a colleague, who fails to ask us why we are upset, or crying, as 'hard' or 'unthinking': we hope for, expect – and deserve – a caring response to our tears.

It is, however, also necessary to ask ourselves whether our desire to 'make better' might imply that the person we seek to help is somehow 'lacking' or 'imperfect', as a result of her – or his – need of help and support. A consideration of this is of great importance. What is it that we mean by the word 'healing', when we speak of the healing ministry of the church? And what is the 'healing' that comes through medical intervention or therapeutic treatment?

While a desire for healing seems natural, and the practice of healing a part of the ministry of Jesus, we have to consider what healing actually means in the life of each individual and of each community. If by 'healing' we mean the removal of symptoms alone, then we are in danger, by associating what *we* perceive to be health and wholeness with what it means to be human, of implying that people who are not 'healed' are somehow *less than human*. And we must be careful not to assume that the limitations, or inabilities, we continue to live with indicate that healing has not taken place or that well-being cannot be experienced.

When seeking ways of caring for others, it is important always to reflect on our motivation, and to consider carefully the effects of any care that may be offered. Our awareness that helping can sometimes create dependence, or that, on occasions, the consequence of helping can be an imbalance of power in which the one in receipt of care feels disempowered and devalued, must be kept in mind. Such awareness, however, must never become a reason *not* to care: it gives, rather, a stimulus to our reflection on *how* to care.

Faith and relationship with God

The story at the beginning of this chapter raises the question: are some people 'unable' to 'have' faith? My six-year-old self saw faith as somehow linked with learning about the stories in the Bible. So, went the six-year-old logic, 'if my sister cannot understand the words in the stories then she cannot have faith'. That, of course, is a very restricted view of what it means to have faith.

I was not alone, however, in thinking of faith as being linked to intelligence or the ability to understand. In the history of the church, ability to recite the catechism, for example, has been a requirement for church membership; and many patterns of worship make it difficult, and sometimes impossible, for people who are unable to read or to think clearly to be able to join in and feel part of what is happening during the church service.

When we reflect on the teachings of the Bible, we see clearly how misguided such an interpretation of what it means to have faith can be. It is because God first comes to us that we are in any way able to be aware of who this God is or to develop any kind of relationship with God. Jesus tells us to 'love one another as I have loved you': the implication is that we are able to know what love is, and how to respond to others in love, because our God has first loved us.

Our Creator knows us before we become aware of God. We read of this in Psalm 22.10, where the Psalmist tells God:

> I have relied on you since the day I was born, and you have always been my God.

Isaiah, too, acknowledges a relationship with God beginning from a time when, in terms of human developmental psychology, he could have had no understanding of faith or of God. Talking to the people of Israel, Isaiah (49.1) declares:

> Before I was born, the Lord chose me and appointed me to be his servant.

Such understanding is deeply embedded in the practice of infant baptism: in the belief that God can – and does – communicate with this 'new creation' even before he, or she, is able to understand. The 'communication channel' is already open, and none of us can have any real idea about what goes on in that special relationship between infant and God. The parents, or those who represent them, may make a commitment of faith, and promise to tell the child, as she, or he, grows, both about the moment of baptism and about the teachings of Jesus. But none of this denies the reality of an already-existing relationship between infant and God.

Refusing to believe that there can be relationship with God without understanding, or without the ability to articulate our faith, reduces God's ability to love to ways in which we can understand or accept. This perception also affects the care we offer. Anyone who does not believe that God can communicate in ways beyond those that seem 'possible' to us is unlikely to see any value in singing hymns to a child with severe developmental problems or other learning difficulties. Neither would they be likely to encourage the woman, whose husband now struggles with the difficulties of dementia, to bring him with her to Sunday worship, as they used to do before his illness began.

For many of us, however, the link between faith and ability to understand remains strong. Years ago, I attended worship in Iona Abbey, along with a group of boys from a residential 'special school', who were spending a week on the Isle of Iona. They were made welcome at the worship, and when it came to the sharing of the bread and wine of communion, I handed the bread across the aisle to one of the boys. It was taken from me from behind, and a voice whispered, 'you can't give him that; he doesn't understand what it means'. [I recounted this experience recently to present members of the Iona Community and was assured that such a response would not be acceptable in the Abbey today].

Well, maybe that boy didn't understand what communion is all about. But do I? Do you? Yes, we have a level of understanding: we may have attended confirmation classes, or have been at Bible Studies where the significance of the bread and wine of communion is discussed and reflected on. But can any of us claim to fully understand? And how relevant is understanding anyway? Our experience of God, as found when we 'taste and see that the Lord is good',[3] is one of the ways in which our God communicates with us. Sharing in the bread and the wine of communion should not be a reward for attendance at church or for ability to understand. Such sharing is, rather, gift from God. We meet with God as we are, and

3 *Book of Common Order of the Church of Scotland,* Edinburgh: Saint Andrew Press, 1994, pp. 139 and 171.

God accepts us, loves us, and directs us in ways appropriate to each of us – just as we are.

People who are experiencing the problems of mental illness are also often denied access to worship or to sacraments because others believe them to be unable to understand and, therefore, take the view that they should not be allowed to participate. I remember the response from one church group that had invited me to speak to them about my work as Mental Health Chaplain, after I told them how, each Sunday, we held a service of worship at which all patients are welcome. 'But why bother', I was asked. 'Are you not just wasting your time? These people cannot think straight. How can they possibly understand what you are saying in the worship?'

Such comments, of course, show clear misunderstanding about mental illness. They also, however, reveal the difficulty created by the view that accepts a link between faith and ability to understand. While not suggesting for a minute that we do not, or should not, make use of the abilities we have to develop either or faith or our relationship with God, we should be wary of linking the two directly. As mentioned above, God accepts us just as we are, and comes to us just as we are. When leading worship in a psychiatric hospital, I may struggle to find appropriate words to help the congregation open themselves to awareness of God and to God's love for them. But this struggle is no more, or no less, than the struggle to minister helpfully in any other context. God, however, has no such struggle! God loves us and cares for us, whatever or situation, and however difficult we are finding it to believe or trust in God. One patient – clearly believing herself unloved and unlovable because of the nature of her illness – came to know this, as she said after worship one Sunday:

> I didn't believe that God would come into a psychiatric hospital. But he did, didn't he? I felt God here. I could ask his help. And I just know he heard me. God still loves me after all! Isn't that great?!

It is indeed. For, if we make assumptions about others, we can deny this opportunity for openness to God. If we say 'this person cannot understand' or 'that person is not able to have faith' then we are denying both the power and the love of God.

Returning to our story at the beginning of this chapter, we can see that I made the assumption that my sister could not understand and that, therefore, she could have no faith. Telling the story helps to highlight how unhelpful this attitude is, and how much it denies the wonderful truth that God's love reaches *all* people.

Faith and healing

Other questions raised by the story concern the relationship between faith and healing, and the meaning of healing itself.

When we look at the account of the healing of the paralysed man — whose friends lowered him through the roof so that he could meet with Jesus – from the perspective of a six-year-old, the answers may seem straightforward:

- the story says that Jesus healed the man and the story says that the man got up and walked: therefore healing = making better
- the story says that because of faith, sins are forgiven: therefore faith = being good
- the story says that the man did wrong (he had sinned) and was forgiven, and then he could walk: therefore not being able to walk = punishment for being bad

Healing is, indeed, about 'making better'. Our belief in God tells us that God wants life on earth to be good. In the stories told in the book of Genesis to help us to understand the origins and purpose of life on earth, we read that God looked at the human beings he had created and that they were 'very good'. Elsewhere in the Bible, we are encouraged to care for those in need and to improve the lives of those who struggle (as, for example, in the passages that tell us to leave enough of our crops for the poor). We are to care for the widow and the orphan and to have concern for the oppressed and the stranger. Jesus, as he calls us to follow his example, describes himself as the one who has come to:

Bring good news to the poor . . . proclaim liberty to the captives and recovery of sight to the blind . . . set free the oppressed (St. Luke 4.18).

Caring for others – a much wider concept than 'healing', as this term is understood in today's medicalised sense – does indeed involve working to 'make better'. 'Making better', however, needs not merely to be understood as bringing about change in the person currently in difficulty. If we are to 'make people better' then *society* must be transformed: prejudices need to be challenged and injustices removed. A man who is unable to walk can be healed when he is viewed as a capable human being, and is no longer spoken to only through the carer who pushes his wheelchair along the street. A woman struggling to balance the needs of her child who requires additional care to the demands of the rest of her family can be 'made better' by the provision of weekly respite care for her child. A young man coming to terms with his diagnosis of schizophrenia can experience a sense of well-being through the respect that is shown to him by mental health professionals and the attitude with which any necessary support is offered.

Understanding healing in this broader perspective puts the responsibility of both 'making better' and 'becoming better' onto the community as a whole. This is a very Biblical understanding of what it means to care. The Hebrew Bible, or Old Testament scriptures, emphasises the community nature of life. It tells us that the love and peace promised by God can come only when all people live at peace and in harmony with all creation. Healing and wholeness are concepts referring to the entire community and not only to the individuals within it.

The image of the church – of the followers of Jesus – as the Body of Christ says something similar in terms of the caring we do. None of us can do everything: we each have a part to play. It is *together* that we are enabled to 'make better': together that we bring about changes that can make whole communities into communities of well-being. Working to create communities of well-being in which all people are enabled and encouraged to live life to the full can be described, in Christian terms, as working to make real the Kingdom of God. This Kingdom is the place where God's love, joy, peace and hope can be shared – 'on earth as it is in heaven'.

None of this denies the reality that there is a relationship between wrong-doing and human suffering. What it does, however, is challenge the assumption that any illness or problem we face directly results from our own wrong-doing. Suffering and struggle are the concern of us all: none of us completely free from either, and all of us have a part to play in the 'making better' of life in the community as a whole.

I need my dog

Most of us struggle when we have to cope alone: we are not made for isolated living. When God expressed pleasure at the creation of human beings, his pleasure included an acknowledgement of our togetherness.

> So God created human beings, making *them* to be like himself.
> He created *them*, male and female, blessed *them* (Genesis 1.27-
> 28; italics mine).

Jesus gathered a group of disciples round him, and the apostle Paul offers us the image of the church as Christ's Body; a body that needs *all* its parts in order to live the Christian life to the full.

As a child, I needed the comfort my dog provided. As carers, we all have our own need for comfort and care. In the church, we think of ourselves as 'carers' or as 'givers'; that is right and proper, since Jesus calls us to care for others. But we must be careful! The risk is there, and often apparent, of creating an 'us and them' divide: *we* are the carers and *they* are the ones who need our help.

All of us need to be cared for, particularly at the beginning and the end of our lives. Some of us require help from others to feed and clothe ourselves. Even when helping people with the most severe of personal difficulties, however, those who give the care often find themselves receiving much from those they care for. Work at a home for people requiring dedicated twenty-four hour care because of their physical difficulties or significant mental limitations can become gift and privilege, rather than mere daily routine, when a hand is held out in recognition, or a touch produces a delighted smile. In my own work as Mental Health Chaplain, I recall spending many hours over many weeks with a severely depressed young man, who was unable to speak or to respond to my presence in any obvious way. But then came the joy of the day when, as I turned to go, he whispered to me quietly, 'please stay'. A moment of wonder for me, and the beginnings of a slow journey of recovery for him.

On many occasions, however, when we offer help or support to someone we perceive to be in need, or someone who has asked for our help, we put ourselves in the position of 'carer who is well' and the other person as 'in need'. While at any specific moment in time that may indeed be the case – the time when our neighbour rushes in and tells us that her husband has just collapsed and died is not the moment to unload our worries about imminent redundancy – we need to be aware that the one we care for *now* is also a person with the ability to care.

Members of the church, immersed as we are in the commandment to 'love your neighbour', can be particularly bad at acknowledging this, and often finds it hard to let the one who has come for help move on. Caring should always arise out of concern for the other, and not from our own need to 'do good'. That we ourselves benefit from the experience of caring needs to be recognised and celebrated, rather than denied. Nonetheless, such benefit should never be the *purpose* of our caring. Our aim, rather, is to enable and encourage a sense of well-being and the discovery of hope in the life of the other.

As we care for others, we can all benefit from our equivalent of a dog to curl up with: the faithful and accepting presence of someone who can 'take me as you find me' and expect nothing from us, except that we are there. Unconditional acceptance, just as we are, gives us the inner resources we need.

Our faith tells us that acceptance comes first and foremost from God. In our day to day experience, though, the reality is that we feel it most clearly in the unconditional acceptance offered to us by other human beings. This highlights to us that, in our caring relationships, most important is that the care we offer shows unconditional acceptance of the other: we care, because he – or she – *is there*.

Some people who are learning to live well, even while coping with mental health problems, have written of their experience in the book *Journeys of recovery*.[4] They mention the importance of being accepted and valued for who they are as significant on such journeys of recovery. One writes:

> This social worker recognised a troubled person, but also my potential, and provided me with the space and continuity to actually build up a relationship. (p. 25)

4 Scottish Recovery Network, *Journeys of recovery*, Scottish Recovery Network, 2008.

Another comments:

> I have been quite lucky. The organisation really pushed me
> towards helping myself... They gave me a bit of choice. Realising
> that there were choices out there was a big step forward . . . A
> number of people offered me extremely valuable support . . .
> [One] supported me in such a way that I could start to believe
> and trust in myself again. (pp. 39-41)

At an event a few years ago to launch the book *Spiritual care
matters*,[5] reference was made to the work of Michael Balint, a
psycho-analyst whose work, in the 1950s and 1960s, encouraged
GPs to appreciate and value the significance of the doctor-patient
relationship in the process of healing. Balint's view that 'the
doctor is the medicine' encourages us, not to deny the value of
medicine, but to emphasise the importance of the relationship
between anyone who seeks to care and the one to whom such
care is offered.

We all have needs. And such needs have to be met be met if
life is to be manageable and bearable. Life, however, is about more
than the provision of the means to exist. Where care is offered out
of genuine concern, and in a relationship of understanding and
compassion, we can begin to think, not just about survival, but
about *really living*. In times of need, illness or distress, the contact
we have with those around us can transform our experience.
Meeting with people who ignore us, misunderstand us, or treat
us as inferior or worthless can cause us great harm, even if such
people can provide us with the means to survive. But where we
discover relationship with those who respect us, who value our
opinions and who take time to listen to our pain or distress, we
begin to discover new life and new hope.

Acceptance by others can change *existence* into *living*. Such
acceptance is what Jesus showed to Zacchaeus the tax collector,
for example, or to the woman at the well. His example is the
one we follow: since all people are loved and accepted by God,
it is our responsibility to love and accept each other. In this way,
the fullness of life that Jesus offers to us all can be celebrated and
shared.

5 *Spiritual care matters: an introductory resource for all NHS Scotland staff*,
NHS Education for Scotland, 2009.

Chapter Three

A Black Person in a White Skin?

Story

A head slowly appears from beneath the duvet under which Friday has been hiding.

The middle-aged man I am visiting was admitted to the hospital yesterday morning. He had not been at work for the past few days and one of his colleagues had called round to see if he was okay, then been so worried that he had phoned the G.P. surgery and requested a home visit. The doctor who went out to see him had been very concerned about the level of his anxiety and distress so had arranged for him to come into hospital. Since his arrival on the ward, Friday has been unable to tell anyone what is troubling him, and has remained curled up in his bed.

I have received a phone call from Connie, the nurse in charge of the ward, asking if I can come and spend some time with Friday. All she knows about him is that he is African, has only been in our country for about six weeks, and that he has been living alone in a room within a unit owned by his employer.

And now I am sitting by Friday's bed, wondering how I can help him. I have been there for a while and, after asking if it is okay to stay, have heard a muffled 'yes' from under the bedclothes. I say to him that Connie has told me he is from Africa and comment that maybe he is feeling very confused, finding himself in a hospital bed in a country he has only recently arrived in. Silence. I tell him my name, and go on to add that I wonder if he might be from Nigeria, since I had met a man there once who was also called 'Friday'. A movement under the covers. 'I was in Nigeria a few years ago', I continue. 'I was only there for a month, so I don't know much about it. But I remember how strange I felt when I first arrived. It was quite scary even though everyone I met made me very welcome'.

It is at this moment that his head appears. Friday shoves down the duvet, props himself on one elbow and looks at me carefully. 'You've been to Nigeria?' he asks. I nod. He seems unsure: 'been to Nigeria?!' he asks again, clearly surprised to hear this. I tell him 'yes' and name the town in the south east of that country nearest to the village I had stayed in. 'Not my part', Friday says. 'I'm from a small small place a long way west of Lagos'.

We sit in a silence that is beginning to feel more comfortable, then Friday puts another question. 'Why am I here?' he wants to know. I explain that all I know is that one of his work-mates had been worried enough to call a doctor and that that doctor had sent him to the hospital. 'Can you tell me about yourself?' I ask him. 'We would like to help you if we can'.

Friday tells me his story. A story that, as I listen to what he tells me, makes me realise just how confused and frightened he must have been feeling. He is quite senior at his work back in Nigeria, he begins. He is based at a factory in a small community far from the nearest large town, and all the senior staff, he explains, are trained in all the various aspects of production. He, however, has been selected by management to come to Scotland to learn about a new production method, and is to return to the factory and be in charge of a special unit now being built there.

The first time he had experienced city life was when he spent the night before his flight in Lagos. He had felt alone there, and suddenly aware how much he was going to miss his family. But he had kept reminding himself of the increased salary he would get on his return, and telling himself that he was, after all, only going to be separated from them for six months.

Since leaving familiar surroundings, life for Friday has become particularly stressful. I listen as he tells me of his experiences: a story of lack of sensitivity and without welcome, that has resulted in his admission to hospital now. His first memory of fear, he tells me, was when he was on board the aeroplane and heard the words over the speaker system, 'we will soon be beginning our descent into Heathrow Airport'. 'I felt really worried then', Friday admits. 'I thought I had got onto the wrong plane. I knew I should be flying to London. Nobody had told me that the airport is called 'Heathrow'.

'And you know what?' he asks me next. 'I found my luggage alright and got through customs okay, but there was nobody to meet me'. I understand his amazement at this lack of welcome for, having been in his country, I am aware of the high priority that is given to the greeting and welcome of visitors and strangers. After some time, he had found someone to ask, and had been guided to transport into London, and eventually found his way to Euston station and a train to Glasgow. But the experience of not knowing and of feeling alone and unwelcomed had clearly affected him significantly.

Sadly, once at work, his problems had increased. He had been sent to Scotland for training. From his experience in Nigeria, 'training' means attending classes and being taught by experts in the field. What he found was that he was being offered 'on the job' training and that he was expected to learn for himself, ask lots of questions and go to the library to learn more in the evenings.

'In my culture, as you probably noticed when you visited us, we do not question our seniors,' he tells me, and I nod to indicate that I had indeed observed this. Friday goes on to tell me how concerned he is that this kind of training will not be recognised when he goes back home. 'I don't even get a certificate', he explains. 'Maybe they will think I have been lazy and not spent my time here learning all I can.'

Not only has Friday found himself in this culture so unfamiliar to him, but it seems that nobody has thought to explain some very different cultural understandings and expectations. According to his understanding and experience, he has not been welcomed and is not being trained in an appropriate way. Other problems appear as he continues his story. He has been provided with a room to live in during his stay, and has access to shared kitchen facilities. But what to cook? And how?

As I listen, I begin to make notes in my head about what help and support Friday might need. If he is to be able to continue to live here and to complete the course that he knows back home is such a privilege and an honour to be chosen for, then those responsible for his training must be made aware of the causes of his distress and encouraged to give him the support he needs.

Having talked all this time about himself, Friday puts another pillow under his head, lies down and stretches. I can see his body beginning to relax, and he asks me to tell him what I think of his country. We talk for a while: about the plantain [type of banana] I enjoyed and the garri [cooked cassava] that I found so hard to eat; about palm trees and village sunsets; about the traditional offering of kola nut to visitors as a sign of welcome and acceptance.

I get up to leave, promising to return the following afternoon. Friday sits up and smiles. 'Thank you', he says. 'And something else.' I pause to hear what else he wants to say. 'Thank you for listening', he continues. 'You know what I think? You're not really a white person: you're a black person in a white skin'.

Reflection

'A black person in a white skin.' That was the way Friday chose to define me: his acknowledgement that – for once in this strange culture which he was finding so difficult to understand and adapt to – he felt that he had been listened to and understood.

In the story that Friday tells we can identify aspects of both Nigerian and Scottish culture. Depending on our experience of industry or of education and training, we will have different points of view about the methods used in each country. What we, as individuals, value most as an indication of welcome will also vary according to how confident or insecure we might be feeling at any particular time. But we can sense how difficult it must have been for Friday, and how frightened he must have felt, to arrive in a new country and find nobody there to greet him and help him on his journey. We can see why he might have felt critical of a culture that does not appear to appreciate the need for welcome and seems unaware of how confusing what is 'normal' can be to the newcomer.

No culture, however, is better or worse than another. There is no 'right' or 'wrong' tradition or culture. Some practices within all cultures deserve praise, and might usefully be adopted by other traditions. Others should be criticised and challenged. At national level, some traditions have become 'bad habits' that are best discarded, just as any bad habits we develop as individuals should be discouraged. Since we do not reject a friend because of his or her bad habits, neither we should criticise a culture or tradition that is unfamiliar to us, just because some of its practices may be less than helpful.

Rather than feeling we must defend what is familiar to us, we need to recognise why it is that those unfamiliar with our culture might feel insecure or fearful when encountering it for the first time. This is true when we are referring to visitors to our country, such as students from overseas, or migrant workers, or asylum seekers: it applies also to making welcome people more used to any environment other than the one in which we ourselves feel comfortable. Holiday-makers unfamiliar with 'the country code' are likely to respond in more considerate ways if they are made welcome and the 'rules' of rural life explained to them, than if they are criticised for their city ways. Rural dwellers, visiting town or city, and feeling lost, confused, or isolated among the crowds, will appreciate friendly advice about directions or public transport.

The same is true when we think about church as a place of welcome. For those of us who are used to the Christian tradition, entering even an unfamiliar church building may bring no sense of confusion or uncertainty. But that is not the case for many in society today, who may know nothing at all about practices considered 'usual' or 'normal' among church members, or for whom the only memory of being inside a church building is of painful feelings of bereavement or loss. As we think about welcoming others into 'our' culture, we must be sensitive to what might seem strange or threatening and so arouse feelings of anxiety or suspicion in the newcomer.

What we see depends on where we are looking from

What we see depends on where we are looking from: it may seem obvious, but it is nonetheless important to keep reminding ourselves of this. Our view of life, and how we understand any issue, is dependent on the perspective from which we are looking. The 'point of view' that we have is just that: the perspective we have from within our own situation and experience. We need to be aware of this as we communicate with other people.

In the story above, we can see how Friday, from his experience of life in a rural part of Nigeria, had a very different expectation of what a training course in Glasgow would be like from what was in fact offered by the company that sponsored it. The real problem, however, was not the difference, but the lack of communication between sponsor and trainee. Had more information been offered, and more questions been asked, most of the distress now being felt by Friday could have been avoided. And had Friday been able to be more open about his lack of experience of catering for himself, or his apprehension about European ways of cooking, more appropriate provision could have been made.

We can see the importance of communication: two-way communication that requires each to listen and to check out that we have heard correctly what has been said, and not merely made assumptions from our own perspective about the words that have been spoken.

As we work together with others in our community, we find ourselves in relationship with people whose background – and, therefore, whose assumptions and expectations – are different from our own. Such variety can enrich greatly the care that we are able to offer, as ideas and experiences are shared. Discussion about how best to meet the needs of the whole community will benefit from hearing from those who struggle most with the problems currently being addressed. They can explain what they would find most helpful or useful, and why. Taking time to listen to their issues and concerns is an important part of our planning, as is the sharing of skills, ideas and resources with mental health workers and others involved in community development.

Bringing together the culture and traditions of the church community with the culture and ways of working with mental health care and local planning, enables the creation of partnerships that can begin to transform the life of any community. But confusion can arise, and tensions develop, if we fail to recognise the difficulties that can occur due to our different understandings and expectations. Good communication is crucial. *Giving* information is not enough: it is necessary to *share* such details in ways that encourage and enable questions and discussion so that points that confuse can be clarified.

Iain Macritchie writes about this need for careful listening and reflection in all communication. Referring to his own chaplaincy work at Raigmore Hospital in Inverness, he describes his role as that of 'translator':

> At one level, there are times when I literally translate the needs of the patient from Gaelic into English, or the requests and enquiries of staff from English into Gaelic. At a deeper level, I am translating Gaelic language and culture (because the two are so inseparably linked) into the language and culture of a modern healthcare community. The aim is always to enable real and effective communication; to increase mutual understanding.[6]

Macritchie's words here point out two issues in good communication. Firstly, that the words we use are closely connected with the culture in which we live. Here, he refers to Gaelic language and culture, but the same need for careful listening, and thus for a level of 'translation', applies in all our relationships. When listening to words spoken by fisherman or farmer, business-woman or housewife, teenager or child, we need to 'tune ourselves in' to what someone living within that particular 'culture' really means by the words they use.

The second issue that Macritchie highlights is that of 'institutional language'. Most organisations develop their own distinctive language, which is accepted within the 'world' of that institution. When used *within* the organisation, this familiar language is commonly understood: those *outwith* it may, however, be confused by the different terminology. Even more likely to cause confusion is the use of words that appear familiar, but whose meaning has been altered from its more common usage.

It may, then, be useful for congregations working in partnership within people from a range of other backgrounds and organisations to become familiar with some of the language used within these other 'worlds'. More important than 'learning another language', however, is to acknowledge the reality of likely differences, and to ask questions and seek clarification at all times.

Such awareness of language and its relationship to the culture within which it is used is just as necessary when we think about the church. We need to remember that many people within our

---

6 Macritchie, Iain, 'The chaplain as translator', *Scottish Journal of Healthcare Chaplaincy*, 1999, 2.2, 7-10, p. 7.

community will be unfamiliar with 'church language', and that the words we use may sometimes conjure up images in their minds very different to the ones we intended. Iain Macritchie refers to:

> the received and approved God-images of the Church and of the Bible as potential barriers to helpful communication.[7]

Being able to 'translate' these words and thus to make them meaningful to others is an important aspect of Christian living within any local community.

Listening and looking: words and images

Before thinking about the language of the church, let us remind ourselves just how confusing words and images can be. Phrases familiar to us in Aberdeen or Aberchirder can puzzle visitors from Galashiels or Girvan. An image that 'speaks for itself' to fishermen from Lerwick or Lossiemouth might seem mysterious to the man in the pub in Kelty or Kingussie.

The words we use can have different meanings according to the context in which they are spoken. Imagine yourself one morning in town shopping. You bump into a friend you have not seen for a while and decide to go for a coffee together. She coughs a little and apologises, saying 'sorry about that; I seem to have a frog in my throat'. You have known each other long enough to understand what she means.

But what about 'mice in my stomach'? What might that signify? The owner of your local Indian restaurant has a married daughter who recently gave birth to her first child. She has not been eating well, and after looking forward to the arrival of the baby, now seems somewhat uninterested in him. Her family worry that she may be sick, and make an appointment for her at your local GP surgery. The doctor invites her to tell him how she is feeling, and she replies that there are mice in her stomach. What is her problem? Is she describing a physical pain? Or might her 'mice' be more akin to what we might describe as 'butterflies', indicative of worry or anxiety? Neither her words alone, nor the image they conjure up in the doctor's mind give much clue. Fortunately for her, this doctor makes no assumptions, and

---

7 Macritchie, Iain, p. 8.

takes the time to ask more detailed questions, until an accurate diagnosis becomes possible. This young woman is describing, in a way that is meaningful in her own language and culture, symptoms of an illness common to many new mothers: that of post-natal depression. Given the opportunity to express herself, within a sensitive and understanding relationship with the doctor, she is able to receive the help and support that she needs.

In our communication with one another, merely *telling* what we have to say, or only *hearing* what is said, does little to create good relationships. Conversation in any household is full of comments such as 'what did you say again . . . ?' or 'what do you mean by . . . ?' When talking with family and friends, we ask for clarification without thinking about it, as we check that we have heard correctly or are clear what we are being asked to do. Such 'checking out' is required in all our conversations: listening to what is said, being attentive to the meaning behind the actual words used and reflecting back what we have heard to ensure that we have understood correctly. Good communication takes time and patience. Without it, confusion can arise, causing tensions to mount and creating barriers between us. Poor communication can result in a breakdown of relationships.

So what about the words that we use in church? How might those outside it understand the 'received and approved God-images' that Iain Macritchie refers to? What is it that we are trying to say when we use them? How might we enable those who come new into our worship to feel relationship with the God we describe in these ways? And how might we make clearer the relevance of our faith to the partners we work alongside in creating communities of well-being?

Biblical images describe God in many varied ways: a few examples are listed here. God is the redeemer of the world (Genesis 1.1; Isaiah 40.28), as well as its creator (Genesis 1.1; Isaiah 40.28). God is eternal, or everlasting (Deuteronomy 33.27; Isaiah 40.28) and is with us at all times (Exodus 13.21-22; St. Matthew 1.23). God is both righteous (Isaiah 45.21) and loving (Zephaniah 3.17; Romans 8.39): he is also portrayed as a God of wrath (Psalm 78.31). God is the rock (Psalm 19.14) on whom we can depend, and who will save all people (Isaiah 45.21; Zephaniah 3.17; St. Luke 1.47).

Jesus, in the prayer that he taught to his disciples, asks his followers to think of God as like a father (St. Matthew 6.9 and St. Luke 11.2).

Such words may encourage people to want to know more about the God they hear described, but they may also have the opposite effect. Picturing God as like a rock might help one man to understand something of the constancy and dependability implied by such an image. His friend, on the other hand, might imagine such a God as dark and dangerous or unheeding.

Having to recite the Lord's Prayer, in which God is described as 'Our Father in heaven' may be so frightening to the woman who was abused as a child by her own father that she is unable to enter into a church building. A different woman, despite having had a similar awful experience of abuse may, however, begin to sense peace and hope, as she discovers that love *can* be offered by a 'Being' defined as 'our Father'.

If we are to help people to be open to relationship with the God in whom we trust, then we have to find ways of describing God that are meaningful and helpful to *them*. This requires us not only to be aware of the effect that specific words may have on those who hear them: we also must be aware of the context in which they were originally used. The words we use in our attempts to describe God need to be both true to the tradition of our faith *and* meaningful to the people around us.

A hymn by John Newton, found in the books used by many different church traditions, contains a verse listing several of the many names used in the Bible to depict Jesus:

> Jesus, my Shepherd, Husband, Friend,
>   my Prophet, Priest and King,
>   my Lord, my Life, my Way, my End,
>   accept the praise I bring.[8]

Names such as these also need to be understood from within the context of the time they were originally used, before they can be 'translated' in ways that help in our community life today.

Jesus himself was well aware of this need to reflect the culture and the experience of the people he talked with. So that the message

---

8 *Church Hymnary*, Fourth edition, Norwich: Canterbury Press, 2005. Hymn number 461. Words by John Newton.

he came to share was to be understood by those who heard it, he used words and images meaningful to them. Frequently, we hear Jesus telling stories – parables – in which he describes scenes or situations that would have been familiar to his listeners. Hearing these stories enabled them to understand the points that he was trying to teach them or explain to them. Through listening to stories of what other people did, or did not do, in situations similar to those they themselves might experience, they discovered more about the life and teaching of Jesus.

The words we speak, the images we use and the pictures we paint of God and of Jesus and of the Christian lifestyle, must be meaningful to those we want to communicate with. Chosen carefully, they can help us to discover, and to share, more about what it means to live a life of faith in God. This is, of course, essential when we are meeting in the context of worship, or discussion group, in which our aim is to enable others to find relationship with God. But it is just as important when we meet outside of the church. A neighbour may be interested to hear about our faith and about why we believe what we do. A friend who has appreciated our help and support may want to find out about prayer.

Being able to talk about God, and about the faith that motivates the way we live, in ways that are meaningful to those unfamiliar with the traditional language of the church, is important not just when talking with people who want to find out more about faith or who seek relationship with God. If we are to build good relationships in our local community and develop helpful community partnerships with people involved in other organisations, then we must be able talk about our faith in ways that can help them to appreciate our perspective on life.

When meeting in a group that is discussing any current issue or concern in our community we, as church members, can explain – in ways that can be understood everyone around the table – the resources we can make available, and in what ways the congregation may be able to help. We expect representatives at such meetings from other organisations to talk in language that we can understand: by choosing our words carefully, we can ensure that they, too, are able to understand the contributions we make.

Welcome and acceptance

Good communication is one of the issues highlighted by the story of Friday. In our reflection this far, we have emphasised the importance listening out for the meaning behind the words we actually hear. We have also considered the need to be aware that way we use language can inhibit as well as enhance good communication.

Our cultural background influences the language we use: it is also the case that the words we use have an effect on the way we perceive the world around us. In any communication, therefore, it is important to recognise the potential for misunderstanding, and to ask for clarification when puzzled or confused or when what is being said seems unclear. The story of Friday's experience is an example of what can go wrong when people fail to recognise this.

Cultural differences, combined with poor communication, contributed to Friday's assumption that he was not welcome. It is clear from what he says that Friday feels that he has not been given the welcome he expected. This does not, of course, mean that he was *unwelcome*. The firm in Glasgow had paid his airfare, offered him training, and had also provided him with accommodation; all this, from their perspective, indicates that they were happy for him to come. His feelings, however, and the difficulties resulting from them, highlight the problems that can arise when expectation does not match reality.

Everyone welcome here?

In any community, however large or small, people need to be welcomed *and* feel welcome if relationships are to flourish. Without such experience of welcome, there is the risk that communication might break down, and that mistrust or suspicion replaces openness and desire for friendship.

We can see this in the story of Friday's experience. The need for welcome was recognised and a welcome was indeed given. The problem arose because Friday and his first contacts in the firm in Glasgow had such different perceptions of what is meant by 'welcome'. As stated above, had either been aware of this, the difficulty could have been talked about, and at least some of Friday's problems avoided.

Unacknowledged, such a sense of not *feeling* welcome can seriously threaten relationships. Friday's new colleagues, unaware that he is struggling to adapt to their culture, fail to offer the help that he had expected. As time goes on, it is likely that, as Friday's sense of isolation continues, his fellow trainees will ignore him more and more, perhaps imagining him to be shunning their company. This experience has the potential to destroy relationships within this present batch of trainees; it could also lead to tensions between staff in the Glasgow office and those in the factory in Nigeria. Worse still, the situation could deepen any prejudice already held, with Friday returning home to speak of Scotland as a country of heartless people and his class-mates spreading gossip that 'all Nigerians' are cold and aloof.

Fortunately, however, his difficulties have been acknowledged. The potential now exists to resolve Friday's problems and to help build good relationships between him and his Scottish colleagues. There is also the hope that lessons will be learned from what has happened. The 'welcoming community' – an industrial organisation on the edge of Glasgow – through its international relations branch, has discovered a new dimension to what it has long prided itself for: a warm welcome to its overseas trainees.

Friday's experience highlights for us the responsibility of the 'welcoming community' – whether that be church or school, Mums and Toddlers or Young Farmers, evening class or 'drop in' centre – in ensuring not only that welcome is extended but that such welcome is recognised and felt.

The words 'all are welcome in this place', when sung during worship, speak of the welcome that should be experienced by anyone who comes into church. The verses of that hymn remind us, though, of the love that God has for all people, and of the need to share that love *wherever* we find ourselves. Whether we are referring to the community of the church or of our local neighbourhood, to our nation or the world, our aim is to build a place:

> where love can dwell
> and all can safely live.[9]

9   *Church Hymnary,* Fourth edition, Norwich: Canterbury Press, 2005. Hymn Number 198. Words by Marty Haugen.

Welcome at our church?

Covid-19 has challenged our understanding of what it means to belong to a church community. Our experience of lockdown has changed the way many of us spend our Sundays. Instead of 'going to church' and meeting together in the church *building*, we have linked up with members of our own, or another, congregation to share in online worship.

The benefits and disadvantages of such 'remote' worship will continue to be debated. What is clear – whatever our views – is that this crisis that we are living through is helping us to rediscover that 'church' means '*people*'.

Finding ways to worship that enable everyone to feel welcome and accepted must be an ongoing priority, whether our gathering together as Christians continues to be physically distant or takes place once again in our church buildings. The need to find new and innovative ways of providing worship has encouraged us to ask questions such as 'is what we are able to offer enabling the people who 'tune in' to discover and share the love of God?' and 'is our time together meeting the needs of those of us feeling lonely or isolated?'

Once we start to ask the questions 'why do we do this the way we do?' and 'how might this feel to someone not used to it?' there will continue to be new issues to consider. Instead of viewing this as a problem, however, it should be seen as a wonderful opportunity. The more we think about what we do – about the way we do it and why – the better it will be done, and the more people will be able to benefit from the resources the church can provide. This is true whether we are talking about the resource of the building as a place of meeting, the spiritual and religious resources found through worship and prayer, or the friendships that develop between us.

Welcome requires us to be especially sensitive to what may seem strange to the newcomer. Details we take for granted can confuse; what we accept as 'normal' – such as standing to sing, or kneeling to pray, or the re-numbering of the pages of the Bible to begin once more at 'one' at the start of the New Testament – may need to be pointed out to avoid causing embarrassment to the visitor. Clear explanation of what is happening throughout a service can help the newcomer to relax and feel part of what is going on. Much planning and thought will be necessary if we are to ensure that *everyone* can participate.

Attention to detail can transform a person's experience of worship from that of outside observer to that of actively involved participant. Changes made, identified originally as necessary to help one individual participate more fully in worship, may be of unexpected value to others. And, importantly, where a culture is created in which new suggestions are encouraged and 'doing things differently' becomes not merely acceptable but the new 'the way we do things here', then more and more people will develop the confidence to ask for what they need. Where such needs are met, people are enabled to participate as fully as they choose to in all the activities of the church.

Our aim should be that *all* feel welcome and that *all* find acceptance and value and a sense of self-worth through the relationships we develop with one another and the care and support that we can give – and receive.

We are all welcome: just as we are. Because God accepts and values us: *just as we are.* Welcome is the starting point out of which relationships grow. Before friendships can be made and trust established, there must be welcome. Before care can be given and received and our interdependence recognised and celebrated, there must be welcome.

Our faith, with 'love your neighbour' as its 'motto', is our motivation. These words of Jesus encourage us and challenge us to welcome and accept one another: *just as we are.*

Shared well-being

Our belief that sharing God's love with the people around us is part of God's plan to bring fullness of life to all people is our motivation to transform our local community into a place of well-being.

Jesus uses the image of salt to help us to understand what this means as we try to 'love our neighbour' as we live in relationship with those around us. 'You are like salt' is what he tells the crowd who have gathered to hear his message. Salt, in small doses is beneficial, but too much salt in our cooking is bad for us, as well as spoiling the taste. Our bodies need salt; too little can be as harmful as too much.

By describing the presence of his followers as like 'salt', Jesus is inviting us to be involved in all aspects of community life. Our role is to offer the perspective of our faith to all our relationships and to all issues and situations that arise. Gathering together for worship and mutual support has a place, of course, but separating ourselves off has a detrimental effect on ourselves as well as on the wider community. We will fail to understand the range of human experience if we relate exclusively to those who share our belief.

Salt is effective only when mixed with a variety of other ingredients. Our faith is an important perspective on community life, but it is not the only one. The abilities and insights, skills and experiences of each member of any community are required: it is as we work together that all can benefit. The well-being of any community is dependent on the help, support and guidance we are able to share with one another.

When describing the church as being the Body of Christ – in other words, as a community trying to live in the way we believe Jesus would wish us to live – the apostle Paul reminds us that, just as a body is made up of many essential parts, so does each member of the church have our own particular gifts that are necessary to the church community as a whole. And just as each of these essential parts of the body is intricately interwoven with the others, so is each member of the Body of Christ linked in inter-dependence with all other members. As Paul puts it, in his letter to the people in Corinth, 'if one part of the body suffers, all the other parts suffer with it; if one part is praised, all the other parts share its happiness' (1 Corinthians 12.26).

Paul is here expressing his understanding of the church as made up of people who are linked inter-dependently each with the other: his illustration of the church as a body, with Christ as its head, is his way of explaining that we follow the example of Jesus not only in our individual lives but also as community of believers.

As members of the church, however, we not only live in inter-dependent relationship with other Christians, but with the whole of humanity. This inter-linking of people one with another is a characteristic of being human and, therefore, of all human communities. As we look around our world, we see how the suffering endured by people in places such as Syria or Afghanistan has been caused by the desire for power and wealth by the already rich nations of the world. And the desperate poverty in which the peoples of Sub-Saharan Africa must live: they are forced to go without, so that we in the rich West can enjoy the resources of their land and the fruits of their labour.

Our own well-being is dependent on the well-being of others, just as theirs is on ours. A community that rejects or ignores some of its members is the poorer for such selfishness or prejudice. Where some people 'have' while others must go without, tensions arise that will threaten the harmony and peace essential to creating well-being among the community as a whole. It is not only those who are excluded who suffer: selfishness also has a detrimental effect on the well-being of those who treat others as of less value than themselves.

One of Jesus' parables, re-told in the Gospel of Luke (St. Luke 12.13-21), makes this clear. A rich man with lots of land has grown too much for his own needs. Rather than share with others, however, he decides to store the grain for when he may have need of it. Even when his barn is full, he does not feel the need to share with his landless neighbours who are struggling to find enough to eat. Instead, he builds more barns, so that he can store more and more. We read here of an attitude very different to the one God asks of his people.

Listening to the 'Parable of the Rich Fool' as this story of Jesus is often called, a young man attending worship in the hospital prayer room had this to say: 'that man is *so* selfish! It's just not fair that people like him are allowed to behave like that'. The young man, clearly angry at the behaviour of the barn-builder in the parable, had more to say. 'And he's not just selfish: he's stupid. He's never going to get a moment's peace: he's going to have to guard those barns in case someone tries to steal from him. He'll even have to stay awake at night to look out for thieves. If only he'd let other people have some . . . then everybody would be okay'.

How right that young man was! By valuing others as much as himself and by sharing with them so that all had enough, that 'rich fool' would have not only helped others but found peace of mind for himself. As we seek to create communities of well-being, there is the continuing need to value and respect each other. 'Love your neighbour' is essential to the creation of communities in which peace and hope can become reality.

Beyond welcome and acceptance

Earlier in this chapter, we looked at how our personal and cultural perspective affects how we perceive other people. We each have our own point of view: what we see depends on where we are looking from. The *reality* in the story at the beginning of each chapter is that a supportive conversation took place between a black Nigerian man – Friday – and a white Scottish woman – myself. In the time we spent together, we were both aware of the difference between us: indeed it was that very awareness that made it possible for help and support to be offered and accepted. Had we denied, or attempted to ignore, our cultural differences, it would have been impossible for either of us to have begun to understand the other's point of view.

In what I told him of my visit to his home country and of my personal experience there, Friday was able to recognise my awareness of cultural difference. Difference needs to be acknowledged and accepted if supportive and inter-dependent relationships are to develop. Describing me as 'a black person in a white skin' was Friday's recognition both of the difference between us and of the potential for understanding to develop.

Communication in which we recognise and accept the different perspective of the other is at the heart of welcome. That is what true welcome means. As we try to make our community into a place where all are welcome, the message we want to make clear is this: you are welcome, just as you are, and here in this place you are accepted, just as you are.

More is required, however, if communities of well-being are to be created. Accepting each other *just as we are* is essential, but it is not sufficient. Loving one another and ensuring that everyone in our community receives all the help and support that is required to live life to our fullest potential is rooted in an attitude of acceptance and of welcome: what is also needed, however, is action to enable growth towards well-being.

Caring for growth: letting go and moving on

Encouragement towards change and growth has two significant dimensions.

The first is part of our 're-active care': that form of caring in which our main aim is to help an individual, or a group of people, who are already experiencing difficulty. This aspect of care is perhaps the one most commonly associated with the expression 'love your neighbour'. It includes practical offers of help, such as preparing a hot meal for a neighbour newly-discharged from hospital or babysitting for a young mum whose husband is working away from home. Emotional support is also a part: listening to the anguish of a recently bereaved work colleague or to the worries of a parent whose teenager is experimenting with drugs.

Sometimes, however, we find it hard to let go of the role of 'carer'. 'Love your neighbour' can be offered in such a way that it is neither the shared activity it is intended to be, nor a recognition and acknowledgement of our mutual need for help and support in a variety of ways. Care and support is not about *doing to* those in need, and thus establishing relationships of dependence. It is about supporting people though times of difficulty and encouraging them to grow and develop.

Let us think, for example, about a young woman, Betty. Betty is new to the area, and comes to church for the first time one Sunday morning. She is greeted warmly, helped to feel welcome and invited through to the hall for coffee at the end of the worship service. She then asks if she can talk with the minister, with whom she then shares her story of marriage break-up, homelessness and subsequent depression, for which she is currently receiving both medication and counselling support. Betty is aware of the importance of getting out more and of making friends in her new community, and readily accepts when the minister offers to introduce her to some members of the Guild. She also agrees to his suggestion that she shares part of her story with a couple of Guild members who are keen to help and support her.

The months go by, and counselling is clearly helping Betty to come to terms with her difficulties and move on. She has felt accepted at the Guild and when an outing is being discussed, volunteers to organise the trip. Is her offer warmly accepted, as her new friends there rejoice in her renewed feelings of self-worth and allow her the opportunity to 'give something back' – as Betty has put it – to the group that has supported her through a difficult phase in her life? Or does a well-meaning, but misguided, Guild committee decide for her that the strain may be too much for her and politely decline her offer for help?

We might ask this in another way: is Betty being given the freedom and encouragement to change and grow, or is the group perceiving her as a 'problem' to be cared *for*? In the latter case, we can see how, although she may have been accepted into the Guild *just as she was*, she has not been given the encouragement that would enable her to grow and move on. Betty is not merely 'a depressed divorcee': Betty is *Betty* and deserves to be accepted not just as who she is, but for who she *is hoping to become*.

Caring for growth: challenge and encouragement

The second significant dimension to loving our neighbour is the more 'pro-active care' which requires us to seek justice for everyone in our community.

If we are to help people towards well-being – to begin to live that 'life in all its fullness' promised by Jesus – then we must do all we can to ensure that they have access to the resources and support that will enable them to do so.

Suppose that, when visiting your new neighbour, Jane, whose elder son is autistic, you hear of the incredible exhaustion of both parents. Not only does the boy rarely settle to sleep before midnight, he is awake and in need of their attention at the crack of dawn. Steve and Jane also have a baby daughter who is going through a phase of sleepless nights. As you listen, you sense that these caring parents are struggling to cope. They had contacted a respite service but were told that they do not qualify for a sitter because Steve's mother lives nearby, and the service gives priority to families without the support of relatives. Both parents know that they could not trust Steve's mother to be alone with either of their children. She has a violent temper, made worse by her excessive drinking, but neither Jane nor Steve feel able to share this information with the respite service.

How might this struggling family be helped, without Steve or Jane feeling dependent, or that they have been identified by the community as a 'problem family'?

On this occasion, an appropriate way forward was found. A member of the local church has a cousin whose daughter has been diagnosed as having autism, and he volunteered to invite the two families to his home to talk about the difficulties of life with an autistic child. A friendship began to develop between the two sets of parents, who decided to write a joint letter to the sitter service asking them to consider adding an additional question to their application form. They suggested that, in addition to asking if relatives lived close by, applicants should also be asked to indicate whether such relatives were able or willing to help and that, if the answer were in the negative, they should be eligible for respite care. Together, they were able to do what Steve and Jane could not bring themselves to do alone.

Loving our neighbour, and helping all in our community towards well-being, means taking time to listen and support each other in times of difficulty. It also means coming together to seek justice. The Bible continually challenges us to seek justice for the widow and the fatherless; in other words, for the most vulnerable members of society at that time. As we seek justice for *all* in our community, we too, must reflect on who are the 'widow and the fatherless' in our own particular context, working to ensure that their needs are met, and that the rights of those who struggle most are given priority.

Welcome and acceptance are not enough: where situations need improving or difficulties resolving, then we must play our part in making such changes. On the journey of life, hope is essential. Acceptance of each other, just as we are, should not deny the possibility of change and of growth towards well-being. Acceptance requires us to weep together in times of difficulty: it also asks that we work together to enable new growth and new hope.

Our faith and the well-being of all

By welcoming and accepting each other, we recognise that we all have value *just as we are*. By going beyond welcome and acceptance, and encouraging growth and change in one another, we enable each other on the journey towards well-being. It is by travelling *together* that we are enabled to use the gifts and abilities that God gives to each of us for the benefit of the community as a whole.

The apostle Paul speaks of carrying one another's burdens. Our aim in supporting each other is to ensure that no-one has to endure more pain or distress than they can endure.

Think of pain relief. Most of us take pain-killers only when pain is causing us discomfort; for minor pain or injury, such a method is appropriate. Some conditions, however, benefit from pain *control*, which is designed to avoid any the horrors of incredible agony. In pain control, medication is administered at regular intervals, the dose having been determined according to the need of each individual.

As we care for others, we might think of our more re-active help and support as being a little like offering a pill once the pain has begun. Supporting a friend or neighbour in difficulty can help make their experience more bearable, and listening to their worries can enable them to identify appropriate ways of dealing with or resolving the problems they currently face.

The more pro-active care of seeking justice that is also so important to our love of neighbour may be likened to ways of controlling pain that aim to prevent its occurrence. Challenging injustice or prejudice can help prevent the awful feelings of isolation or despair experienced by people who feel themselves unwelcome or rejected.

Carrying one another's burdens inevitably means sharing in their pain. But as Paul reminds us, although it is indeed the case that 'if one part of the body suffers, all the other parts suffer with it', it is also true that, 'if one part is praised, all the other parts share its happiness'.

As Christians – again quoting words of St. Paul – we are to 'be happy with those who are happy', and to 'weep with those who weep'.

On the journey of life, we are – as individual Christians and as a congregation together – to remember that our way of life should be as the gospel of Christ requires.

The faith of the local church is important to the life of the whole community. As we participate together in helping those who need help and supporting those who need support; as we recognise our own needs and turn to others for help; as we challenge injustice and ensure that the voice of those who are vulnerable is heard, the motivation of our faith enables the well-being of all.

Living together, acknowledging the gifts we each have as well as the difficulties we all face, and recognising our inter-dependence one with another, can bring meaning and hope to the community as a whole.

As disciples of Jesus, who came to show people how to live, we seek to make the gifts of God's Kingdom real in the lives of all people *now*.

Where inter-dependence is not merely recognised, but celebrated and enjoyed, more and more people are enabled to discover a life of meaning and of hope. Pigeons may never swim, but lives previously filled with darkness and despair will find freedom and hope as wings are stretched and new possibilities identified.

Chapter Four

If only . . .

Story

It's late on a Thursday afternoon and I'm heading back to the psychiatric hospital after a visit to one of the day units. Squeezed into a seat near the front of the bus, I am thinking about a conversation I have just had with one of the men at the unit. I've known Jimmy for almost a year by now, and we have talked about all sorts of issues together: problems he has had with the Housing Department, his childhood in the south of England, the current political situation. But I am conscious that, wherever our conversation starts, he always returns to the same theme. On every occasion we meet, at some point during our time together, he will pause in what he is saying, and, with a sigh, continue, 'if only I could see that heron again. Then everything would be all right. If only . . . '

As on so many previous occasions, I ask myself 'why?' Why is this heron so significant to Jimmy, and how can help him to discover that the future – and, indeed, the present moment – could be as good and as fulfilling as that day when he saw the heron seems to be for him. It's not as if we haven't talked about this. Today is far from being the first time that we have sat together and wondered 'why?'

As I sit on that bus, I ask myself the same question again – 'Why?' My thoughts roll on: 'Why is that experience of Jimmy's *so* special for him? And 'if only . . .' *what?* What is so wrong with Jimmy's life now that he has to keep returning to a special moment from his past? Are there no special moments for him now? And if there aren't, then is there anything we can do or say that will help Jimmy? Anything that will enable him to feel good in the *present*, rather than constantly believing that good feelings are only to be found in a return to the past?'

Sometimes Jimmy seems as perplexed as I am. When life is going well for him, I can, as I listen to him, sense his frustration with himself. At these times, it is *he* who asks the 'why?' question, and he sounds annoyed with himself as he asks it. 'I don't *want* to be always talking about it,' he says to me. 'I don't even know what I would do if I saw a heron here. It just keeps coming into my mind, though. That wonderful feeling of calm I had when I saw it. I sometimes think I'd do *anything* to feel like that again'.

At other times, though, it seems not so much that thoughts of the heron are 'coming into' Jimmy's mind, but that the heron has taken up residence in it and is preventing him from thinking about much else. On such occasions, I am not the only one to be fearful for Jimmy. During really bad times for him, he has been brought to the hospital by his neighbour who was terrified that Jimmy's desperation to see the heron again may lead him to kill himself rather than continue living without it. Sometimes, it seems that Jimmy's 'if only . . .' is threatening to destroy him.

Reflection

Jimmy's story may sound extreme. His continual desire to return to the past, with its conviction that 'if only' that heron might reappear then all will be well, is making it difficult, and sometimes almost impossible, for Jimmy to deal with the routine ups and downs of day to day life. His longing for an experience that is past is clearly adding to his difficulties in the present.

Looking back with fond memories, or wishing for 'another go at that' so we could avoid mistakes made earlier, however, are not uncommon desires. Few of us would claim never to have lain awake at night wondering why we did what we did, or what made us blurt out that remark in the way we did; wishing and wishing that we could have that moment again, so that we could get it 'right' this time around. We all have our own 'if only . . . s'. Most of the time, however, with daylight comes the realisation that life goes on, and that we cannot turn back the clock. If we have made a mistake, we must accept it. If we have had a wonderful time, then, yes, let's remember it. But if we want to enjoy ourselves so much again, we must get up and go to work, and earn enough to afford such leisure time. Life goes on!

Life goes on: but it's not always easy

But we also know how difficult it can be – this 'getting on with life'. Imagine yourself sitting up late one night, full of regrets at an argument you had earlier that day with your neighbour, and wondering what to do now. Should you just forget the whole incident? But if you do that, then what will you say when you bump into her on the street? Would you apologise then? Will you phone up? Or would it be easier to write? Or do nothing at all?

Suppose it is more serious: what has happened may have put your job on the line, or caused a real split in family relationships. And it seems like your fault. A simple 'sorry' will not, it seems, repair the damage; so what do you do? At times like these, when difficult decisions may need to be made, or tough consequences faced up to, it is important that we have the support of a caring friend or neighbour.

The more difficult the situation, the harder it is to know how to deal with our feelings about it. We may want to forget; to block out the past and move on. But the memories keep coming back to haunt us. We may find ourselves longing that the past could be revisited, as we go over and over in our mind what we should, or could, have done, while at the same time wishing that we could just forget the whole thing and get on with life.

We all have regrets and we all have longings: longings for a better past as well as for a more hopeful future. Jimmy's longing, however, is at risk of overwhelming him. It is when our focus on the past inhibits our ability to live in the present, and prevents us from having hope for our future, that significant problems can occur.

In this chapter, we will look at how various aspects of regret and of longing can get in the way of day-to-day living, and thus create problems for our mental health and well-being. We will also consider how we might help one another to move on from negative feelings about what is past. Such moving on may involve a change of attitude, or of behaviour, or both. It will be necessary to accept the reality of what has happened, before we can find ways of changing our patterns of relating or our ways of behaving. We may also need to challenge whatever it was that caused, or contributed to, the problem, to ensure that such difficulties do not have to be endured in the future, by ourselves or by others.

Longing for the 'good old days'

Why might we find ourselves looking back to the past with longing? There will be almost as many answers to that question as people who experience such feelings; but perhaps we can identify a few key features.

Most of us will have heard an elderly relative or neighbour comment that 'things just aren't like they used to be.' Listening to my own grandmother's stories of her 'good old days', in which so much of her time was spent in washing clothes by hand, and setting the fire each night so it was ready to be lit the following morning, I found it hard to imagine that memories of such hard work could be good ones. As a teenager, with neither time for nor interest in the domestic essentials of life, I thought she should be glad that she now lived in a compact, cosy flat with a gas fire and a washing machine. What I realise now, of course, as I struggle to learn about digital television and the workings of my new laptop, is that, while what she did in her earlier life may have been hard work, it was, at least, familiar and predictable. 'What will I do if the machine breaks down?' was a question that caused my grandmother more stress than any amount of washing and wringing. Not only that, but her longing was not *really* for the hand-washing and the coal collecting: it was for her family, now grown up, and for the companionship of neighbours on the back green on washing days.

This kind of longing for the past can be helpful. Where we remember with fondness, and try to keep alive the community traditions of days now gone, such memories create a sense of continuity, both in the life of an individual and in the life of the wider community. In any society, those who remember 'how things used to be' have an important role to play, not least in reminding planners and policy-makers that change is not *always* for the best and that 'new' does not always mean 'better'. Memories of the past are an antidote for 'change for change's sake'.

Where memories and longings for the past get in the way of positive change, however, they can, of course, do harm to both individual and community. Were the voice of the past to dominate any society, it is hard to imagine that progress would be made – new education ideas created, community health initiatives developed, or rural health networks put into place.

Communities need encouragement to develop, and to become places of well-being. There has, therefore, to be a balance between reflecting on the experience of the past and focusing on the reality of current situations, if the needs of the present moment are to be met.

The same is true for individuals: we need to balance our memories of the past with our hopes for the future, if we are to make the most of life in the present moment.

Back to 'normal'

Longing to be 'back to normal' is a feeling most of us will recognise. When the children go back to school after the long summer holidays, or our visitors wave to us as they set off home, or we pack away the Christmas decorations, we may sit down with a sigh, and say, 'ah well, it's back to normal again'. At such times, what we mean by 'normal' may have little to do with whether what we now experience is 'better' than what we have just been doing. It could be that 'back to normal' is felt, at least at first, as somewhat of a let-down, or a disappointment, after the freedom of summer holidays or the fun of having visitors to stay.

Getting back to 'normal' can also be experienced as a sense of relief. Entertaining guests and making special meals is often stressful, and it is comforting to return to 'auld claes an' porridge'. And for many, the Christmas season can be a difficult time of year, with its expectation that we all 'must' enjoy ourselves. Getting 'back to normal' means a return to routine, and to all that is expected: a sense of familiarity and of security. 'Normal' is not necessarily enjoyable, or full of meaning or of hope: 'normal', for most of us, is reassuring and safe.

Sometimes, however, our sense of longing is rather different. When life is difficult, or painful, or distressing, we wish – quite understandably – that this were not so, and may find ourselves longing for a return to 'how it used to be'. When going through a time of illness, or learning to cope with an unavoidably difficult situation, we may find ourselves looking back to a past that, from our present perspective, appears infinitely better, if not ideal.

When struggling to cope during a time of mental illness, the desire to 'get back to normal', or longing for life as it used to be, involves more than our longing to be free of symptoms. We may long to feel safe and secure, or to be with people we know well and can trust. It can be difficult, and add greatly to our distress, when, for example, our home and all that is familiar is on the island of Harris, but treatment for symptoms requires a stay in hospital in Inverness.

Even when medication removes distressing symptoms, though, a return to life, *just as it used to be*, is unrealistic. The experiences of life change us: admission to hospital, being perceived as 'vulnerable', or having to be more dependent on others all affect how we see ourselves. To go back to how life was before *any* experience – good or bad – is not a realistic expectation. Nor is it what most of us really want: the 'return' that we hope for is less a longing to go back to life as it was, than a longing to be free from, not just the symptoms, but also the consequences, of illness or distressing experiences.

Focussing on how life was 'before this struggle' is often unhelpful, and can even contribute to the experience of mental distress. Longing for the past can be a denial of present reality. Constantly referring back to 'how things used to be' can also prevent us from dealing with the present. If all our energy is going in to remembering, and trying to re-create, what our life used to be like, then we will have few resources left to face, and so to deal with, the reality of our present situation.

Thinking back to the past may also be an indication of our desire to *feel* 'normal'. During times of mental illness, it may be that we feel little control over our emotions, and such lack of control can make us feel very vulnerable. We describe depression as 'descending on me like a huge black cloud' or anxiety as 'taking me over completely': such expressions indicate our vulnerability, as well as our fear, at such loss of control.

Those struggling to cope with mental illness may also long to be 'back to normal' in the way others relate to them: 'normal', in this sense, implies being treated with respect and being included and made welcome. People who face stigma as a consequence of their mental illness may long for the 'normality' of acceptance. Not being noticed, though itself a form of prejudice, may be preferable to being abused or ridiculed.

Seen in this way, 'normality' is something that we can offer to people in our congregations or in the community around us as they go through a period of mental illness. We ask a neighbour how she is coping since she had her knee operation, when we call in to welcome her home from hospital. Although visiting that same neighbour, when she is recovering from a period of mental illness, may be something we feel more anxious about doing, it is important that we overcome any hesitancy we may have: she needs our friendship and support as she struggles to cope with prejudice from others as well as with her pain.

Talking about the reality of their present difficulties is, therefore, beneficial to most people experiencing a time of mental illness. Spending time with friends who accept what we are going through, and who want to understand us and support us, can help to make the reality of our present distress more bearable. Knowing that someone else is present with us in this reality can give the confidence, or the courage, to begin to look through our pain, and beyond into a more hopeful future.

Special moments

A return to his life, as it used to be, however, is not the main focus for Jimmy. His concern is, indeed, with the past: much of his conversation, as outlined in his story at the beginning of this chapter, expresses his desire to return to a past experience. His longing is not to return to the daily routines of his earlier life, nor even the desire to get back to life as it was before his first admission to the psychiatric hospital. Jimmy longs to repeat one specific special moment; to re-live that moment and to re-experience the wonderful feelings he associates with it.

If Jimmy is to help himself through his present difficulties, and to benefit from the support he is being offered, he has to face up to the reality that this experience can never be repeated. As mentioned in his story, there *are* times when he is very aware of this: he well understands that even were he to return to the same river where he once saw the heron that had such an impression on him, it would not, almost certainly, be the *same* heron; and his changed circumstances mean that it is most unlikely that he would experience *now* the same feelings as he experienced all those years ago. And, even if he could, would they mean the same to him now?

Jimmy needs support and encouragement as he asks himself 'why?' 'Why is this heron *so* important to me? *What* was so special about the feelings that seeing it created within me? And *why* do I long to feel *that* emotion – again and again?' Once he can begin to find answers to these questions, the longing will begin to lose its control, and Jimmy will be able to devote his emotional energy to dealing with his present situation.

When life feels chaotic, it is, of course, understandable that we should want to hold onto an enjoyable experience, or to a moment of calm.

Think of a young girl, whose parents are addicted to drugs, living in poverty in a high-rise flat. She struggles to get herself to school in the mornings and often does not make it. And when she does, she is so tired and hungry that she cannot concentrate. Then her class is taken on an outing. After their tour round the castle, there is a picnic, and a burn to paddle in, and she plays, feeling the warmth of the sun on her back. She wishes she could stay there for ever.

Or imagine yourself feeling totally out of control; problem after problem is weighing you down, and it seems like decisions are being taken out of your hands. 'Everyone and his Auntie' appears to know exactly what would help you, and the opinions of neighbours and church friends are whirling round inside your head. You long just to close your front door on them and your worries, as you remember the power you felt, as a teenager, when you marched into your bedroom and slammed the door.

Trying to re-capture, or re-live experiences, however, is not likely to help us through our present difficulties. Nor is looking over our shoulder, with longing, for a past that is gone. A story from the Bible may help us here. This story, of the Transfiguration of Jesus (St. Luke 9.28-35), stresses the importance of living in the present, not in the past. It also, for those of us with faith, helps us to see more clearly the inter-relationship between our faith and the way in which we live our lives.

The story is about Jesus, who has climbed up a mountain to pray. Three of his disciples have accompanied him and, while up there on the mountain, they have a special moment of awareness of the presence of God with them. The physical appearance of Jesus seems to change. Then both he and his disciples hear the voice of God telling them that Jesus is indeed the special son of God, and that the disciples are to listen to Jesus, to learn from him and to follow his example.

According to the accounts of the Gospel writers, these disciples of Jesus had earlier left behind their families, their friends and their work, in order to be with Jesus and to hear his message. There must have been moments, as they followed him, when they asked themselves 'why?' – 'why did I do this? What on earth made me leave my job and my security?' And now, suddenly, they are given this moment of certainty. God speaks directly to them: God answers all their 'why?s' as he tells them that Jesus is his son, and that they are indeed to follow him.

No wonder they wanted to hold on to that moment! It must have been so amazing that they thought that, once it has gone, they might find it almost impossible to believe it had ever happened. They wanted, not just to remember, but to set up a memorial, so that each time they come back up that mountain, they would have evidence of that special moment. No doubt, they also hoped that each time they entered the monument that was erected, they would re-experience the moment, and that, once again, God would speak clearly to them.

We may not long to hear the voice of God in such a way, but would any of us deny ever longing to feel *sure* about our faith? How good it would be to know for certain that what we are planning is what God want us to do. How reassuring to know that the decisions we have just taken at Presbytery, or church meeting, will, indeed, best serve the needs of our local community.

Moments of certainty, however, according to what Jesus says to his disciples, are not to be held onto. Rather than looking back to them, we are to move on from them. Such special moments *do* have a purpose: they reassure us of God's presence in our daily routines, and of his guidance as we care for one another. What needs doing *now*? Do it. Trust in God: get on with living. As a hymn found in the Methodist Hymnbook puts it:

While here we kneel upon the mount of prayer,
the plough lies waiting in the furrow there.
Here we sought God that we might know his will;
there we must do it, serve him, seek him still.[10]

For Jesus, the special moment is over. Coming down from the mountain, Jesus meets again with the crowd that has gathered to hear him, and heals a sick young boy.

As Christians, what we see in this story is how the special knowledge given to the disciples that the man they follow is indeed the promised Saviour has no purpose in *itself alone*. Its purpose is to offer the *assurance of faith* that convinces them of the need to *share the love of God* with all people. Jesus came to bring new life and hope to all: his followers must seek to do the same.

Taking risks and finding opportunities

If we never had regrets, would we ever want to change? If we never made mistakes, would we ever learn? If we never missed an opportunity to do something we really wanted to, or to do what we knew to be right, would we ever be motivated to do better next time?

Realising where something went wrong, how a mistake was made, or when an opportunity was missed, can help us to make choices and decisions in the future. The past, inevitably, affects both present and future. *How* that past influences us is, to a certain extent, a choice we can make for ourselves.

As parents, responsible for the well-being of our children, we may want to protect them from a sense of failure or the pain of making mistakes. We do all we can to avoid that risk. And, of course, it is important to encourage those who are young, or with less experience: if they find themselves always failing, or always coming last in any game or competition, they may give up trying, and grow up with a very poor self-image. But think of the child whose parents make sure he *never* loses at a board game, or the mother who *always* ensures that her daughter comes first when they have a race in the park. How will these children react when

10 *Hymns and Psalms: a Methodist and Ecumenical Hymn Book*, London: Methodist Publishing House, 1983. Hymn number 158. Words by Samuel Greg.

they go to school and discover that they are *not* the faster runner in their class, or that they do *not* get every answer right? Such parental contriving to ensure their child never fails is not only denying the reality of life, that none of us can be good – let alone best – at everything; it is also denying them the opportunity to grow and to learn.

Accepting that what we do *now* will have consequences for both present and future is a necessary part of development. It is a part of taking responsibility for our actions, both as individuals and as members of the community in which we live. Those refusing to accept responsibility for the choices they make may find themselves rejected by the community around them. The freedom to make choices is an important dimension to our humanity, but so, too, is the acceptance of responsibility for the consequences of the choices we make.

We can take care that we do not deny anyone – ourselves included – the opportunity to grow and learn through the choices we make. Of course, where any individual is particularly vulnerable and in need of constant care, we must do all we can to ensure that he, or she, is protected from any hurt or harm. *Over*-protection, however, reveals our lack of ability, as carers, to give a person the opportunity to learn and grow through mistakes or regrets. It may say more about our desire to be perceived as caring than it does about our concern to offer the care and support that is *actually needed*.

To take all decision-making away from anyone who is in some way dependent upon our care risks denying their humanity. God created us as people who are to make choices: choices about how to live, choices about how – and indeed whether – to live in a way that acknowledges our relationship with the God who created all things.

Even where the decision to be made is the most basic, we recognise the humanity of the other, and the potential that God has given to each and every one of us to grow and develop, by enabling each other to make choices for ourselves.

For people whose understanding, or level of awareness, is extremely limited, choice may, for example, mean indicating with a glance, or a point, that orange juice, rather than blackcurrant is the drink that is preferred, or screaming when music is played that is not wanted. Such decisions should be respected, and the ability to make them acknowledged. Each human individual, as created by God, with his or her unique abilities, and unique contribution to life on this planet, has the right to respect. Encouraging this freedom to choose reminds us, as carers, of the unique needs of a unique individual. Such encouragement also opens the way to growth and development.

Significantly, too, offering this freedom to choose reveals the common humanity of carer and cared for: we are *all* God's children, and are helped to recognise this as we discover the importance of *choosing* in the development of our self-identity. To assume that Bill wants to drink blackcurrant juice today, just because on every day for the past week he has taken it from me, or to assume that, because Agnes lay contentedly while that CD played last time means that she wants to hear it again, is to deny our shared humanity.

The comments above, on enabling *all* people, whenever possible, to have the freedom to choose, stress the significance of choice in the development of self. Choice and self-worth, and choice and taking responsibility for ourselves, are part of being human. To deny ourselves a more fulfilled future, whether out of regret for past poor choices, or reluctance to risk new ones, is to build roadblocks on our journey to well-being.

Guilt

A sense of regret is often associated with our awareness of the part we ourselves had to play in recent events. There are times, however, when we find ourselves looking back with regret that something has happened, without either any feeling of responsibility, or the conviction that had we made a different decision, things might have worked out differently. Something has happened, and though we may wish that it had not, we know that we had no responsibility for the difficulties it may have caused.

A feeling of *guilt*, however, implies that we feel responsible for what has happened.

The word 'guilt', as it is commonly used, indicates that some wrong-doing has occurred. Collins Westminster Dictionary defines 'guilt' as 'the fact or state of having offended; criminality and consequent liability to punishment'.[11]

Thought of in this way, a person feeling guilt is aware of having done something wrong, and aware, too, that there will consequences for such wrong-doing.

We do not, however, have to commit a crime in order to *feel* guilty. Most of us know the pain of guilt, yet have never even contemplated breaking the law.

Here, we are not thinking about the relationship between guilt and the law. We focus, rather, on the *feeling* of guilt, and the effect it can have on our life and the life of those around us.

Guilt is a natural, and healthy, response: to feel guilty leads us to change for the better, to repair any damage caused, or to ask forgiveness for any hurts inflicted. Awareness of guilt can help us to deal more appropriately with future life experiences than we have done in the past. Feeling guilt, although painful, is a powerful force for personal change and growth. Coming through an experience of guilt can lead to new insights and new hopes for our future.

Frequently, however, guilt is experienced very differently and, instead of reflecting on its cause, then seeking to make amends, we feel weighed down, and incapacitated by the burden of guilt. For many, the idea of guilt is so bound up with that of punishment, that the possibility of moving beyond guilt without some form of punishment is beyond their ability to imagine.

Sometimes, struggling to cope with problems related to mental illness, a feeling of guilt may be one problem too many. Guilt for being ill, for not being able to contribute to the family income or to care for our children, gets in the way of improving our situation. Such guilt, far from being healthy, has a negative impact on our health, and we find ourselves in a downward spiral. Illness creates its own problems; guilt exacerbates them. Guilt can numb and immobilise us, leaving us worse off than symptoms of illness alone would warrant.

Guilt about being ill is not easily removed. Like all other emotions, we feel what we feel, and while others may encourage us, and assure us that we have to need to feel guilty, such advice does little to take the feeling from us.

11 *Collins Westminster Dictionary*, London: Collins, 1966, p. 231.

Much more important than merely being told we need not feel guilty is to change the perception of mental illness within society. Without improved understanding by the wider community, individuals who experience periods of mental illness will continue to feel guilty, just because they are ill.

A sense of acceptance by others, and of being valued for who I am, even within the experience of mental illness, can make bearable any guilty feelings I might have.

A young woman, apparently content, in one of the wards in the psychiatric hospital where I was working as Mental Health Chaplain, borrowed a cigarette-lighter from a visitor and later tried to set fire to herself. She sat on the floor and put the flame to her socks which, fortunately, did not burn well, and before any fire could take hold, it was quickly put out. Her feet and ankles required treatment for minor burns, but the woman was otherwise unharmed. What had led her to attempt to end her life in this horrific way? Guilt. She felt guilty simply for being alive. She had first experienced an episode of mental illness in her late teens, and was aware how disappointed her parents were that their hopes of her going to university were, apparently, not to be fulfilled. Problems had recurred, although she had times of feeling well enough to work, but her family had made the decision that she should remain at home with her parents rather than risk the pressures of more independent living. She felt responsible for letting them down; she believed herself to be a burden to them; she felt guilty simply for existing. Death seemed the answer.

Fortunately for her, help was available and, although her parents were naturally distressed at this attempt to end her life, they were able, in the way they responded to her, to show her just how much she meant to them. They told her – and showed her – that they loved her, and always would. Well, or ill, she was their daughter. Their unconditional acceptance of her, alongside the medication and the counselling she received, enabled her to regain a sense of self-worth and self-acceptance. The feeling of guilt did not leave her completely, but it was no longer all-consuming. As her emotional energy increased, bit by bit she became able, not only to cope with day to day life, but to make plans for her future.

When guilt is all-consuming, or preventing us from being able to participate in day to day life, it is tempting for those concerned about us – whether family or friend, or professional carer – to persuade us that our guilt is neither appropriate nor necessary. While these words do, indeed, often apply to the guilt experienced, such persuasion is rarely helpful. As stated above, what we feel is what we feel: no amount of persuasion can 'switch off' our emotions. Not only that, but few of us can ever claim to have *nothing* to feel guilty about. All-consuming guilt is indeed unhealthy; it needs medical treatment as well as care and support.

Just because guilt may be excessive, though, it does not mean that *no* part of it is warranted. To tell someone – however well-intentioned we may be – that they have *nothing* to feel guilty about makes it almost impossible for them to say 'sorry' for things they know only too well they *are* responsible for. To deny that opportunity is not only unhelpful: it is to deny the humanity of the other. We all have the need – not only the need but also the *right* – to make amends, to apologise, or ask forgiveness and to move on. It is these actions that make it possible for us to live at peace with ourselves and with those around us.

Guilt and faith

Guilt that is unhealthy needs to be identified, and anyone suffering from it given the help and treatment that may be needed. It is very different from the sense of guilt that can encourage changes in attitudes or behaviour, restore broken relationships and lead to health and well-being. This form of guilt I refer to as 'God-given gift'. It is a feeling that stimulates us to move on; to reflect on wrong things done, or bad decisions taken; to apologise and make amends.

For those with faith, this restoration to right relationship applies also to relationship with God. As we care for others in our local community, this means being sensitive to any belief *they* may have, and to the understanding they may have about God's relationship with them. Whichever name a person uses to address the 'Being' whom we, as Christians, relate to as 'God', when we offer care or support, we should take time to listen to how their faith may be affecting their feelings of guilt.

We need to be aware, too, of how *our* understanding of God and his relationship with us might influence how we view guilt and forgiveness.

Believing that God is primarily a God of love, who understands the temptation to do wrong, we are likely to hold the view, outlined above, that guilt is a God-given gift that *motivates* us to change. Since God is always ready to forgive, unconditionally – as expressed in the Parable of the Prodigal Son (St. Luke 15.11-32) – we speak of forgiveness first, and only then talk of making amends. If, on the other hand, we have been brought up to believe in a God of anger, we may be more inclined to see guilt as punishment. This view of God may lead us to tell others that freedom from guilt must be *earned:* behaviour must change before forgiveness can be given.

It is important that we reflect on our own perceptions and understandings so that, as far as is possible, we do not let them get in the way of offering to others what is most appropriate to their present need. Sharing our beliefs, when people are struggling with feelings of guilt, can be beneficial, but care must be taken. Our personal interpretation is just that; personal. It is necessary, therefore, that we meet together in reflection and Bible study, not just to increase our *own* knowledge and faith, but to help us become more *sensitive* and *appropriate* in our caring for others.

In the chapter *Only One Magpie*, we will focus on another important issue: the need for knowledge of both the *context* in which any Bible story was recorded and of the *present situation* of the person to whom such a story is told. This is of particular relevance as we consider the potentially disabling experience of guilt. Told out of context, passages of scripture, liturgy and hymns or songs can confuse, or even harm, those who are weighed down by guilt.

Nonetheless, where feelings of guilt are experienced in relation to some wrong-doing, or to thoughtless or selfish words spoken, support and encouragement is needed, while forgiveness is sought or restorative action is taken. Words from within the tradition of the church, carefully chosen, can be helpful in enabling people to 'wipe the slate clean and begin again'.

Used sensitively and appropriately, words rooted in the Christian tradition can help people, weighed down by the pain of guilt, to feel forgiven, both by God and by those they have wronged.

Fundamental to knowing this forgiveness, however, is the acceptance, support and encouragement that we offer. Being accepted, whatever we may have done, is what enables us to forgive ourselves.

Shame

A sense of shame is different from the experience of guilt. Shame is focused on the self as being 'bad'. 'I ought not to be here', or 'I should never have been born' are ways of describing the feeling of shame that many people experience.

When something that we have *said*, or *done*, is acknowledged as wrong, or misguided, we can change our behaviour, accept forgiveness, and be freed from our guilt. Shame, however, makes us feel that we, ourselves, *are* bad. With little, or no, self-respect, and feeling worthless and unacceptable, people who live with a sense of shame are in especial need of on-going care and acceptance. For how can anyone live life *well* while believing that they are, simply by being there, *bad*?

Stephen Pattison, a practical theologian currently living and working in Birmingham, in his book about pastoral care and shame, notes that the word 'shame' can be traced back to an Indo-European root word meaning 'to hide', or 'to cover oneself'.[12] We sense this desire to hide away from others in comments such as 'I just wish a big hole could have opened and swallowed me up' or 'I could have died when I heard him say that'.

Shame is intimately related to our sense of self in relation to others. Feeling ashamed means believing that it is myself as a *person* – rather than what I have done – that is 'bad'. This suggests that shame may be similar to what has been described above as 'unhealthy guilt'. The young girl, mentioned above, who tried to set fire to herself, used the word 'guilty' to describe her experience of life in relation to her parents. Another person might, though, in a similar situation, talk of feeling shame; of feeling ashamed of himself or herself, just for being there.

---

12 Pattison, Stephen, *Shame: theory, therapy, theology*, Cambridge: Cambridge University Press, 2000, p. 40.

Shame can be one of the consequences of stigma. Commonly, such shame arises from being associated with a group perceived to be 'different' or as people to be feared.

A young man, beginning to find ways of coping with his diagnosis of schizophrenia, goes out to the snooker club with his mates. Lads at the next table are arguing about who might have carried out a recent attack on a local street, and one of them declares, 'it'll have been one of them schizos that did it, I'll bet'. And the young man feels ashamed.

A child watches a recording of a news item made about her.[13] She was born with Down's Syndrome, and the programme is about foetal testing. The interviewer looks across from the mother he is interviewing to her daughter, then says to the camera, 'this is one that slipped through the net'. As she watches, the girl feels ashamed – just for being alive.

As we try to help those who feel shame, it is our acceptance of them *just as they are* that is so important. Our aim is to encourage people to value themselves; to accept themselves and to develop a sense of self-worth and hope as they discover meaning and purpose for their lives.

Moving on

To live well, we need each other. Feeling ashamed, we need acceptance. Feeling guilty, we need forgiveness. Jimmy, as he learns to accept that there can be no return to the past, needs support and encouragement.

We cannot experience well-being merely through determination to 'move on'. Jimmy's longing to feel 'calm' – as he felt when he watched that heron so long ago – is real. However much he wants to forget the past and move on, his need to feel calm, to live free from the anxiety that is causing him so much distress, must be met. Practical help will be needed, as well as encouragement, if Jimmy is to live *well*.

Supporting people for whom their past has become a burden, or whose memories of the past are limiting their present potential, is an important aspect of our pastoral care. But caring is about

---

13 The interview with this girl's mother was shown on Channel 4 television news, Tuesday 16th September, 2008.

more than support. We also work together to ensure that whatever has brought pain and suffering in the past will not continue into the future. We challenge prejudice and do all we can to ensure that no-one in our community need continue to feel ashamed of who they are.

Journeying together

'Today is gift: that's why we call it the present' is a familiar saying that is helpful in reminding us of the importance of seeking well-being *now*.

As Christians, thinking of each day of our life as a 'gift', we sometimes speak also of the 'sacrament of the present moment'. Each moment is special. Each day is a day in which God's love can be experienced. Each day is a day in which God's love can be shared.

Loving our neighbour is about caring *now*. Caring for one another is about accepting each other – just as we are.

But loving our neighbour is also about *journeying together*. It means helping one another to accept our past, and to recover from the pain and the hurt it may have brought us. It means helping one another to move on; to lay aside our regrets and to look forward with hope. It means accepting one another, not only 'just as we are'; it also means supporting one another as we change and grow.

'Yesterday is history and tomorrow is mystery'. These words, part of the saying quoted above, are also relevant here, as we think about life as a journey to be travelled together, and of loving our neighbour as lifelong commitment.

Saying that 'yesterday is history' does not mean denying what has happened in our lives, but it does mean recognising that what is done is past. That is what forgiveness means. As we accept forgiveness, and are able to forgive ourselves, we learn to love ourselves 'warts and all'. Offering forgiveness to others, we are freed into relationships that encourage our well-being.

We do not ignore tomorrow, just because what will happen is still 'mystery'. Plans are made, and learning from past experience can help prevent problems in the future. Thinking, together, about what is needed now if life is to be lived well, can help make our dream of community well-being become reality.

Loving our neighbour, as we journey through life together, is about helping each other to accept what is past. This sharing in the journey of life, as we care for each other, is also about planning together for a future in which *everyone* can experience well-being.

Journeying together is about helping one another to live *well*, as we care for each other, day by day. It is about working together to create communities of well-being in which God's love and God's justice can be shared by us all.

Chapter Five
Halfway to Where?

Story

People are beginning to gather in the community room. It's almost 11 o'clock and time for the weekly discussion group in the Half Way Home. I am living here for a few months, while learning about mental health care in India. Every week at this time, residents and staff meet together for this opportunity to talk about any topic of interest to the group as a whole.

There is a blackboard in the corner, on which details of planned outings or other arrangements are sometimes written. As we come in today, however, I notice that a sentence has been chalked onto the board. It reads: 'Faith is [gap] able to move mountains [gap] gives us strength to climb them.' I am still thinking about what has been written, and wondering about the two gaps in the sentence, when Amith comes in. He looks at the message then crosses to the board, picks up the chalk and puts the words 'not' and 'but' into the two blank spaces. 'Who rubbed out what I wrote?' he asks, with a hint of anger in his voice. There is a pause before Meera answers. 'It was me,' she says. 'Because you put that faith can't move mountains but it can.'

I am unsure whether Amith has put his message on the board, hoping it will become this morning's topic for discussion, or whether he wrote what he did specifically to annoy Meera, for the two always seem to be arguing about something. 'Faith can't *really* move *anything*', challenges Amith, but Anita speaks up in support of Meera. 'Oh, yes it can,' she asserts. 'It says so in the Bible.'

By now everyone has arrived, and Meenakshi looks around shyly. She is the appointed community leader this week, and so it is her responsibility to start off the discussion and make sure that everyone who wants to join in gets the chance to do so. She is clearly uncertain how to begin: I sense her considering whether

71

she should let the conversation continue or ask for other discussion topics. She looks around thoughtfully, watching the expressions on our faces, and then comments, 'I feel we all want to carry on talking about this. Am I right?' Some voice their agreement. Others nod their heads. A few appear to have no interest in helping to make the decision.

Discussion, once people begin to express their ideas, becomes lively and occasionally heated, but Meenakshi is a calm and effective group leader and everyone has the chance to air their views. Someone describes faith as weakness, saying that expecting faith to help us is just like being dependent on others instead of coping on our own. In reply, he is told that faith can help us because God's help makes us strong.

Soon, however, the focus moves from faith to the mountain. There is general agreement that the 'mountain' we are talking about represents a problem. What do we do when we find a mountain blocking our path? What do we do on life's journey when we are confronted with a problem? 'Tackle it', say some. 'Climb up it. That's the only way to the other side.' 'I'd try to go round it,' says a young woman sitting near the window. 'Only a coward would do that,' comments an older man, 'a strong person should climb up to the top.'

The young woman is upset by what he says. 'Are you saying I'm a coward? Don't you think life is hard enough? Why make it more difficult? If there is a way *round* a problem isn't that less painful than fighting my way through it?'

'Climbing to the top is best,' someone else asserts. 'When you get to the top you can see where to go next. If you get a clear view it's easier to decide what to do.'

'That's okay if you've only got one problem. If the view after tackling it is good. But what about me? I've got so many problems. If I climbed up all I would see from the top would more and more problems. If I don't climb up, then at least I can just worry about what is closest. I don't *want* to see all the other problems lining up like the Himalayas ahead of me – on and on and on. What kind of life would that be?'

Life as a journey, with problems that loom like mountains in our path, is an image that stimulates a lot of ideas. It also produces a considerable amount of emotion within the group. We reflect on how whether we imagine ourselves climbing up the mountain or walking more cautiously around the mountain depends on the kind of person we are. And recognise that we might tackle problems in different ways, depending on the kind of problem we are facing.

We talk, too, about what can help along the way. Food. Water. Appropriate footwear. And we think about what these might represent in relation to coping with problems on the journey of life.

The discussion goes on, and I find my mind wandering from these images of walking in the hills around Vellore, here in south India, where my biggest worry when exploring them has been the lack of trees for shelter from the blazing heat of the sun. I think about the mountains of Scotland, and all I have learned about safety in the hills. Be prepared. Don't go alone. Take a map. And a compass. Tell someone where you are going – and keep to that route. If weather conditions deteriorate, retrace your steps and return.

As my thoughts return to the room and the discussion around me, I realise that not one person has said that they would turn back. Or ignore the mountain. Admit defeat. The talk is all about coping with problems and about finding ways of continuing the journey. That's great, and I sense the shared desire to move on: residents working hard at developing new skills, while learning how to cope with the realities of life lived with a mental illness. But I also worry that so much of the discussion is about struggling to cope alone; about travelling the journey of life independently, with no mention of support from others.

No one has spoken of asking for help. Or of travelling with a companion. I am surprised by this, since, here within the Half Way Home, people are almost always willing to help each other. And residents have shown amazing sensitivity and thoughtfulness in helping me to adapt both to Indian culture and to the routines of the Home. I wonder: perhaps it is the image of 'mountain' that is closing off discussion about travelling *together*. Mountain climbing is not, given the heat and the barrenness of the rocky hills around here, a local pastime. Most, if not all, in the group are trying to imagine an activity they have never actually done. Everyone is aware of the reality of problems and the need to face them or work through them, but the mountain-craft skills that I have grown up with are unfamiliar. Nobody sees that retracing steps is wise self-care and not failure. Or that never going alone indicates a sense of responsibility, and is not a sign of weakness.

A different image might have been more useful in encouraging the group to think, not only about finding the inner strength to cope with our problems, but also about helping and supporting each other on the journey of life.

Meenakshi points out that it will soon be lunch time, and asks if anyone has anything else to say before the meeting ends. Meera reminds the group of the words on the blackboard that had started the discussion, stating again her belief that faith can, indeed, move mountains and so can take away our problems. Several others, including Amith, disagree loudly. 'You're not talking about *faith*,' says Amith. 'That's just wishful thinking!' Then he goes on, more quietly and thoughtfully: 'why should we expect problems to disappear? If there were no mountains, there would be no valleys and rivers and flowers. If we keep worrying about problems, we'll never feel better. Maybe we should think of mountains not as *problems*, but just as *there*. And that faith can help us see the whole picture'.

'That's an important point, I think', says one of the counsellors. 'Life is not always full of problems. I know being ill can be hard. But everyone in this room has things you are really good at; not just problems.'

His colleague agrees, 'That's right. We need to remember what we *can* do as well as the things we struggle to cope with. I know my faith helps me. I guess "faith" means different things to different people, but for me it's not just "wishful thinking". More like 'encouragement from somewhere else' is how I think about my faith'.

The bell for lunch rings and one or two people begin to stand up, so Meenakshi brings the discussion to a close, suggesting quietly, 'maybe next week we could talk about faith'.

Reflection

This story helps us to continue our reflection about life as a journey. Not only does the discussion consider life in this way, but members of the group are living in a Half Way Home, the very name implying that they are in a 'between' place: a place of transition between what has gone before and what is yet to come.

The residents in that place are all people who, after being diagnosed as having a mental illness, have found it hard to continue living at home with their families. Because they have been struggling to cope at work, or to contribute to family life in a useful way, someone in their family, or perhaps their doctor, has recommended that they come to the Half Way Home.

Some of the staff are also resident there. They are trained in counselling or social care, and are, therefore, able to offer appropriate help and encouragement. Additional support is offered by other members of staff, who come in to teach skills useful in building relationships and finding employment. The hope is that time spent in this place, in which mental illness is recognised, and in which those who experience its difficulties are accepted and helped – not stigmatised or rejected – will enable those who come to live here to adjust to living within any limitations resulting from their illness. As residents are encouraged to care for others, as well as for themselves, their self-confidence is restored, and they are enabled to re-discover a sense of value and self-worth. Through *being* accepted and valued, those who live there begin to *feel* accepted and valued, and so discover, or re-discover, a sense of meaning and purpose for their life.

Words and images: what do we mean?

The very name of the home invites questions. Half way from what? And half way to where? Where were the residents before they came to live there? What is this 'half way' place that is their current experience? And where is it that they are headed? These questions are at the heart of the reflection in this chapter.

As noted within the story, we see that images portraying life as journey may be more, or less, helpful, depending on our experience of life. Taking time to consider the relevance, or otherwise, of images we ourselves find helpful, is necessary, therefore, if we are to help other people come to terms with *their* experiences.

This need for awareness and sensitivity in our use of images is also relevant when we talk about God, for here also the words and images we use can help, or hinder, other people. Words and images convey a variety of meanings, which differ according to our culture, experience and emotional state.

In this chapter, we also think about what is meant by the terms 'mental health' and 'well-being', from the perspective of our understanding of health and from that of our faith. How can we live with a diagnosis of mental illness – or with any other difficulty – while also experiencing a life of mental health and well-being? Can we live with illness, or other problems, at the same time as living the life 'in all its fullness' promised by Jesus? And is such 'fullness of life' the same experience as the hoped-for aim of health care services – mental health?

These, and other, questions are looked at in this chapter. As church members, trying to create communities of well-being, they are important questions for us to consider. An over-emphasis on distinguishing between the Biblical promise of fullness of life, and the aims of health and social work professionals trying to improve people's mental health and well-being, can inhibit the positive value of working together in our communities. Insisting that there is a 'better' – more fulfilling – way of life than people may be able to imagine, or be ready to accept, will alienate, rather than help and support, those within our communities who may be in most need. And denying any distinction at all can lead those outside the church, as well as ourselves, to question the value and the purpose of our faith.

What the Bible teaches us about life – life as it is and life as it can become – is an important contribution to any discussion about well-being, and a useful guide in any planning made or actions taken. The priority it puts on seeking justice for all people needs to be heard and responded to, just as much as does its emphasis on caring for others and loving our neighbour as we would wish to be loved ourselves.

Working together in our communities to make them into places of well-being means, of course, listening to the ideas and advice of professionals who have particular skills and experience, as well as to the concerns and priorities of those most in need of help. But working together also requires that we share *our* experience and knowledge: that we tell of what faith teaches us about inter-dependent living and about sharing the love we believe is God's gift to all people.

Halfway living

The home featured in the story above is in India. The concept of 'half way' accommodation, however, is also found in our western culture. Our society also offers 'half way' meeting places, such as day centres run by health or social work services, and self-help groups organised by people who recognise the value of coming together and supporting others living with a similar illness or difficulty. The negative aspects, as well as the more positive benefits, of such 'half way' support will be looked in this reflection, as we consider the question 'half way to where?'

What might life in a half way home might feel like? For some, such a place can offer security and a refuge, both of which are important dimensions to life for us all. A weekend away from the responsibilities of caring for our family; a day out walking along the sea shore; curling up in bed with a romantic novel: we all have ways such as these of giving ourselves a break from busy-ness and stress. Even taking the phone off the hook can offer the refuge or respite that we need. Undoubtedly there can be value in the care and support that 'time out' in a half way home can provide.

But this does not mean that life there is easy. I remember asking one of the residents in a home, similar to the one in the story above, but here in Scotland, what would be most helpful to her at that particular point in her life. 'Not to be here in this place', was her reply.

What was it that made her want to get away from that place? What was her experience of 'half way' life? Was she feeling ready and able to be going out to work, or wanting to live alone in a flat? Did she have a family, or a partner, looking forward to her returning to live with them? She may have been frustrated at having to share her daily life with other people experiencing problems similar to her own, or have felt herself no longer in need of the more sheltered and protected environment.

One of the hopes, certainly, of those who work in half way homes is that the people who come to live there for a while will be able to identify for themselves when they have reached the point when they are ready to leave and move on. However clear, or unclear, we may be about the destination, or even the next step of the journey, what *is* clear is that a half way home is not intended as a permanent address. Implicit within both name and concept is that residence in a half way home is temporary: a kind of 'staging post' between life as it used to be and life as we would like it to become.

Wanting to get away from such half way living, then, or reluctance to move into a home in the first place, may sometimes be stimulated by feelings of uncertainty. 'How long will I be allowed to stay?' Or 'how long will you make me stay?' are questions likely to be asked. 'Is there a level of "wellness" that will be required before I can leave?' And, if so, a person might feel considerable anxiety, as they wonder if they will ever be able to 'achieve' such wellness; anxiety likely to prove detrimental to any longed-for change or development.

Another difficulty a resident in a half way home may struggle with is in coming to accept that they need help. The symptoms of mental illness are hard enough to have to deal with: acknowledging them, and being expected to listen to the advice or suggestions of others, may add to the level of distress and vulnerability already felt, however necessary such support might be.

There are, though, significant benefits to living in a half way home. Acceptance by others sympathetic to the difficulties currently being endured. Time away from the stresses and strains of our usual environment. Protection from the prejudice of those without the patience or the willingness to accept us and our problems. Help from trained staff: support through any immediate crises or problems as well as help offered in preparation for the next stage of our life.

There is, however, a significant disadvantage within any 'half way' experience, whether residential or not. And that is its built-in assumption that it is the ones currently experiencing illness who are the ones who need to change. Of course it is the case – as with any aspect of life – that when experiencing the problems associated with mental illness, there are ways in which we can, and must, help ourselves. But by separating people from the rest of our community, the message being given out is clear: they are to 'improve' or 'get better' before they will be welcome within the wider community.

While acknowledging this, it is also the case that being given the opportunity to meet together with other people facing similar difficulties to ourselves can give enjoyment and a feeling of safety, as well as providing support. Many of those who attend day centres are, with justification, angry at any suggested closures. These centres are places where friendships are made, as well as support given, and a range of activities provided. While nobody, of course, should prevent, for example, a woman from enrolling at the local community flower-arranging class just because for years she has been struggling with depression, the reality is that this can be a hard thing for her to do. A more understanding approach might be to ask that class tutor to offer a few sessions in the mental health day centre.

Whatever our accommodation, we live in a local community. It is not where we live, but the *attitude* of others that causes us to feel accepted or rejected. We all need to feel welcome and accepted. Some of us may spend all our life in the one place; others may have to move to a new community for employment or family reasons. Some of us, too, at some point in our life, may require the benefits that a more carefully focussed, more supported kind of 'half way' experience can provide. When we do so, we should still be welcomed and accepted, not rejected or forgotten. We should be cared for and loved, not only because we are vulnerable or in need, but because we are part of the community. Because we belong. Because we *are there*.

'Social inclusion' or 'love your neighbour'?

Well-being cannot be experienced in isolation from other people. Feelings of wellness and of illness influence, and are affected by, the relationships we have with those around us. Pain that feels unbearable when faced alone can become bearable when shared. A decision can be made calmly when our wife is at home to listen as we mull over various possibilities: making that same decision may seem an impossible challenge when we are required to make it alone. And isolation can spoil even the most pleasant outing or activity.

The reality of human inter-dependence means – although, of course, there are times when it is satisfying and enjoyable to spend time on our own – that we need the presence of others. Not only that but, as highlighted in the *Prologue*, we live in inter-dependent relationship with our surroundings, both natural and humanly-designed. Pleasant surroundings may help us to experience a sense of well-being: difficult living conditions, on the other hand, can increase or even cause the problems that make us suffer pain or distress.

Writing in a textbook for social work students, Steve Hothersall – senior lecturer in social work at Aberdeen's Robert Gordon University – has this to say: [14]

> Good mental health . . . include[s] a sense of being well adjusted to and attuned with the environment . . . Because human beings are social animals, good mental health extends to our relationships with others.   Isolation, loneliness, lack of belongingness, social exclusion . . . are all attributes of or contributors to poor mental health.

Feeling that we do not belong can damage our sense of self-esteem. The child who is prevented from joining in a game can feel excluded from the group. The teenager who is avoided at school because he enjoys doing craft-work, or the student who is made fun of because she attends the church youth group, can feel rejected and worthless. Not feeling accepted in our workplace, or not being invited to a family celebration, can undermine anyone's shaky self-confidence.

Feeling ourselves accepted and welcome is hugely important to our mental health and well-being. Acknowledgement that everyone in society has the right to be welcomed and accepted is important: 'social inclusion' policies are intended to challenge attitudes that hinder such acceptance. Prejudice against those perceived, for whatever reason, to be 'different'; abuse of those who are vulnerable; hatred stimulated by bigotry or religious fundamentalism; racism: all these need to be confronted if we are to live peacefully together in communities of well-being.

But is a policy of 'social inclusion' the answer? Can policies stop one person from ignoring another? Or prevent feelings of hatred? It is, of course, possible to bring in laws that make illegal the acting out of such feelings in ways that harm other people. Our 'rights based' society encourages those of us who have the confidence to do so to stand up for such rights. But do we really *feel* more valued and accepted by knowing that, as a person with a history of depressive illness, we have the *right* to equal employment opportunities? Or that, because we are unable to hear, we have the right to demand that our local church installs an induction

---

14 Hothersall, Steve, et al., *Social work and mental health in Scotland*, Exeter: Learning Matters Ltd, 2008, p. 6.

loop system? Will our insistence upon these rights make us more accepted and welcome? And what about the many of us who are not able to demand such rights?

The very concept of 'social inclusion' as policy assumes that there are some people in our society who have the power and the influence to do the including. So, who are the 'we' who do the including? And who are the people that this 'we' invite 'in' to 'our' community?

On one level, this seems quite straightforward: if I move in to the house next door to yours, and you ring my doorbell to say 'welcome to the neighbourhood', then you are quite reasonably acknowledging that, at this moment in time, I am the one who is the newcomer and you are the one who is able to extend a welcome to me. Acceptance offered to one individual by another *just because they are there* can ease entry into any new community and often marks the beginning of new friendships.

But suppose you have been to a meeting in your local community at which it has been decided that there should be a policy of social inclusion. You are all invited to think about the people living in the houses near to where you live; might there be someone feeling unwelcome? You think about this and, having noticed – but have previously chosen to ignore – that regularly every fortnight I receive a visit from the Community Psychiatric Nurse, you decide that I may be someone who needs to 'be included'. When you come to visit me, I may be relieved that, at last, someone has made the effort to make contact, and welcome you into my home. But, especially if I sense that your visit has arisen, not out of genuine interest, but out of a sense of duty, my reaction may be more hostile. I do not want to be noticed, or included, because of my need for support. I want to be welcome for *who I am*.

If we are not careful, a policy of inclusion can create the very divisions that we are at pains to remove. In the example above, in which you and I were meeting as individuals, there is hope that any tension might be resolved. Unless you have come *only* so that you can report back at the next meeting that you have done so, and have no interest whatsoever in me as a person, it is likely that the visit will prove beneficial. Working to include specific *groups*, however, implies the need first to identify and categorise. Such labelling can be counter-productive, for we are all, first and foremost, *individual people*: our identity should never be defined by a category such as 'disabled', 'housebound' or 'lonely'.

An over-arching policy that ensures rights, and enables access to facilities and appropriate care or support is, of course, essential. 'Social inclusion' is, as a principle, important. It must, however, be pursued with caution, if we are to avoid creating unhelpful divisions within local communities. We need to recognise that everyone living in our community is *already* 'in' – because they are *there*. And that awareness of the specific needs of each individual is what is required, not merely a policy for the group of 'them' that any individual is perceived as being a part of.

Let us consider two specific examples. First, let us imagine that the village hall committee, realising that access to activities held there is impossible to anyone who requires to use a wheelchair, decides to install a ramp. An important decision has been made, not only because legislation demands such access, but also because several local people who previously could not get into the hall are now enabled to do so. We must not devalue the significance of this. Yet we must also recognise that merely providing a ramp is not enough. Alex is an elderly man who lives on his own and, outside of his own home, needs a wheelchair to get around. But he no longer has the strength in his arms to propel himself as far as the hall. What use is the new ramp to him?

A second example is this. A church meeting has made the decision to open up the hall each Wednesday morning to welcome mothers with babies and toddlers. Plans to start this group had begun after a concerned church member became aware of several new families in the community in which the adult male in the household was regularly working away from home on the North Sea oil rigs. She felt that young mothers would appreciate the chance to meet up with other young mums who were spending much of the time alone with their children. As indeed they did. But what nobody noticed was that one young mum was missing out. Each Wednesday, Dorothy left the village early on the first bus, in order to reach town in time for a meeting of the Post-Natal Depression Group. Although benefiting from being part of that group, she was missing the opportunity of meeting up with *local* mums, and was being left out of the informal invitations made during 'Mums and Tots' at the church hall – simply because the others did not see her there. Not only was the local group failing to help Dorothy, its existence was contributing to her sense of isolation.

'Love your neighbour' is the way to welcome and acceptance of everyone in our community. Jesus' answer to the question 'who is my neighbour?' is clear. My neighbour is not just the person like myself. Nor is my neighbour only the person I like: we are asked to love our 'enemies' as well as our friends. The definition of 'neighbour' has no limits. We all live in this world together. Because you are there, you are my neighbour: because I am here, you are mine. Supporting each other on the journey of life, as we recognise our inter-dependence, each upon the other, can lead us along the path sign-posted: *towards mental health and well-being*.

What is 'mental health and well-being'?

We may agree that it is difficult for anyone to be healthy or to feel a sense of well-being while living with pain. And acknowledge that freedom from suffering can restore our hope and thus bring a sense of well-being. But as we do this, we also recognise the difficulty of identifying precisely what is meant by the terms 'mental health' and 'well-being'.

Our understanding of these words is likely to differ according the situation we currently find ourselves in. A general sense of our own well-being can be challenged by feelings of panic, as we face a critical audience, or by nausea as we push ourselves towards our physical limits to make it on to that mountain peak. Often we recognise these pressures as 'normal ups and downs': in other words, we perceive well-being not as a fixed state, but as fluid and changing. It is usually only when difficult feelings continue, or adversely affect our ability to relax or to sleep, that we may begin to think about our mental health, or recognise our need for help or support.

What one individual views as mental health can differ from the perception of another. A young man, for example, when re-visiting his doctor to discuss his medication, may be perceived by her as having significantly improved mental health, while he feels himself to be struggling to cope, because this change in his medicine is making him feel more drowsy and less able to concentrate. He may, therefore, appear to others to be 'better', while in himself, he is feeling 'worse'.

Another doctor, from a reading the case notes of a new patient, may expect to hear from her that life is a real struggle. And yet, when he meets with her, and listens to how she describes herself, he discovers how she has learned how to deal with the emotional ups and downs caused by her illness. She tells her doctor about the benefit that attending regular a relaxation class has brought and talks about the new friends she has made since joining it. Thus, though her symptoms are of 'illness', the woman's experience is that she is living well and enjoying new relationships.

In a book entitled *Whose reality counts?*, Robert Chambers emphasises the importance of responding *appropriately* to *real need*. A change in attitude is required: not merely the provision of services.

Chambers offers the following definition of 'well-being':[15]

Well-being can be defined as the experience of good quality of life . . . [W]ell-being is open to the whole range of human experience, social, mental and spiritual as well as material . . . Extreme poverty and ill-being go together but the link between wealth and well-being is weak or even negative: reducing poverty usually diminishes ill-being, but amassing wealth does not assure well-being.

This is helpful in its reminder to us that well-being is not simply defined through absence of illness. Well-being is more than freedom from mental illness, just as, according to the World Health Organisation, health is:[16]

a state of complete physical, mental and social well-being and not merely the absence of disease

Chambers' words are also helpful in making clear the relationship between poverty and ill-health and, thus, highlighting the social and political dimensions that are so important to mental health and well-being.

---

15 Chambers, Robert, *Whose reality counts?: putting the first last*, London: I.T.D.G. Publishing, 1997, pp. 9-10.

16 World Health Organisation definition of 'health'. See https://www.who.int/about/who-we-are/constitution (accessed 13/8/2020).

By suggesting that well-being implies a quality of life that is 'good', however, his definition raises questions. How is 'good' defined? And by whom? The answer to the question in the title of this chapter – *Half way to where?* – may, ultimately, depend on our understanding of what it means to have a *good* quality of life.

What is suggested here, and throughout this book, is that how we live is less about what we *have* and more about what we *are*. What we discover, through our Christian faith, is that life is about *being*. Such understanding is fundamental to our motivation to create communities in which *all* can develop in ways that lead to the discovery of mental health and well-being. We live within inter-dependent relationships in which all people are accepted and valued, just because we *are*.

John Swinton, Professor of Practical Theology at Aberdeen University, points out this relational dimension to mental health and well-being in his description of mental health as: [17]

> a complex process of psychosocial and spiritual development, that may or may not involve the eradication of specific mental health problems . . . [M]ental health is viewed in terms of a person being provided with adequate resources to enable him or her to grow as a unique individual and to live humanly as persons-in-relationship.

Many factors affect our mental health and well-being. While our personal experience and our feelings about such experience are vital in determining whether we are mentally healthy or not – no one can tell anyone else what they 'must' be feeling – there are some broad indicators of what might encourage mental health and what might inhibit it.

Scottish Government policy recognises the complex range of factors that affect our mental health and well-being. A study undertaken on its behalf identified a set of positive influences on mental health, found to be shared across different age groups and community groups. These positive influences were listed as: [18]

17 Swinton, John, *Resurrecting the person: friendship and the care of people with mental health problems*, Nashville: Abingdon Press, 2000, p. 135.

18 Scottish Executive, *Building community well-being: an exploration of themes and issues*. Project Report to the Scottish Executive prepared by the Scottish Development Centre for Mental Health, 2003, p. 5.

- relationships: family, friends, company and social contact
- social activities, entertainment, hobbies and interests, exercise and sport
- advice, information, reassurance
- access to support and services
- money – to enable people to maintain self-respect, keep warm and clean, have a nice house, feel comfortable . . .
- feeling that you matter and have a role, are useful and are able to make a contribution
- choice and involvement: feeling involved in decisions that affect your life and the lives of those around you, having your views heard and respected
- having hope, feeling valued, having a sense of progress and future prospects for yourself, your children and grandchildren

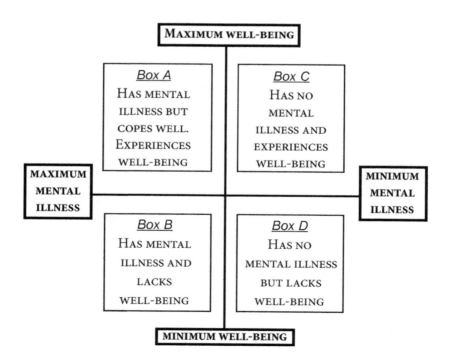

- feeling proud of what you are part of, what you have achieved individually and collectively
- confidence and self-worth: opportunities to learn and develop skills (not just academic skills)

Mental health, and the sense of well-being associated with it, is about far more than the absence of mental illness.

The diagram opposite[19] highlights some important aspects of the complex relationship between health and illness. It shows how it is possible to have a diagnosable mental illness while enjoying positive mental health. It also points out the reality that we can live with no diagnosable mental illness and yet experience poor mental health and have no sense of well-being in our day to day life.

Thinking about the life experience of individuals from the perspective of these four 'boxes' in turn can help us to see where, and how, the church might be of most help on the journey towards well-being.

In <u>Box A</u> we find those of us who have a diagnosed mental illness but are coping well and have good mental health. This experience – of a sense of well-being despite mental illness – is possible because of a variety of reasons:

- understanding from others
- acceptance by others
- lack of prejudice from others
- sense of self-worth: encouraged by a), b) and c)
- positive relationships
- good support network
- accessible and appropriate care and support
- sense of meaning and purpose
- sense of hope even in times of difficulty

From this list, it is clear that mental health and well-being is not something that we can 'have' or 'not have' in isolation. Being diagnosed with a mental illness, we may require medication or other therapeutic treatment. What is also necessary, however, is the care and support of family or friends.

---

19 Diagram adapted from *Mental health in the workplace*, Scottish Development Centre for Mental Health, 2004.

None of the ways listed above that can encourage a sense of well-being are restricted to what the church can provide. Good community relationships and friendships offer them all. The church, however, can share in helping to provide these means of help and support. Indeed, we not only *can* help here, but, if we take seriously our commitment to following God's way of love and compassion, then indeed we *must* do so.

For those asking questions about the meaning and purpose of life, or struggling to feel a sense of hope in their lives, discussion about faith, an invitation to attend a church-based group or to join in with worship in the local church may be helpful. And where such hope may seem impossible, due to the circumstances currently being endured, then, as emphasised throughout this book, the church has the responsibility to work together with other agencies to ensure that injustice is challenged and the needs of all people in any community provided for.

In Box B, we find those of us who have a diagnosed mental illness and who, for various reasons, are unable to feel any sense of well-being. These reasons are likely to include a lack of any or all of the positive points listed under Box A.

Stigma or prejudice can undermine our sense of self-worth, and struggling alone without the support we need can make living with hope seem an impossible dream. Life can become a nightmare in which the problems of mental illness and isolation from others lead to feelings of hopelessness or despair.

People experiencing life in this 'box' are in particular need of care and acceptance. While those in Box A have been able to find at least some support and help, those in Box B have, for a variety of reasons, been unable to do so. Struggling, alone or unaided, with not only mental illness, but also with the prejudice that so frequently accompanies it, can leave a person devoid of meaning and purpose. Unemployment or homelessness add to such feelings and can remove any sense of self-respect. Circumstances, combined with the thoughtlessness or prejudice of other people, can leave us feeling desolate and unable to make contact with the very people who might best be able to help us. Human relationships are thus crucial to re-creating a sense of self-acceptance. More than anything, when we feel somehow 'beyond help' and less than human, it is relationship with another that can rekindle hope.

Being there – doing what is necessary but, much more than that, simply *being there* with the other – is how despair can be transformed into hope. 'Being there' is how God cares for us: our 'being there' with others is how that care is made real.

In <u>Boxes C and D</u> are those of us who have no diagnosable mental illness. Some may be fortunate in living with this experience throughout our life, but for many of us, such freedom from mental illness will be a phase that we move in and out of. Many of us may experience a period of mental illness at some point during our life.

Even when free from any symptoms of mental illness, we can experience poor mental health. Living without any of the benefits in the list above can leave us feeling isolated or without a sense of purpose. Moving away from home to work or study can make us feel vulnerable or uncertain, thereby inhibiting our enjoyment of and interest in such new challenge or opportunity. Finding ourselves freed from the responsibility of having teenage children around our home can produce 'empty nest' feelings that lead us to wonder what meaning our life will have from now on. Changes beyond our control, such as being made redundant from work, new regulations that reduce the hours we can spend at sea fishing, or disease in the herds we have raised, can leave us feeling tense and anxious.

When circumstances challenge our sense of well-being, we need the support of family, friends and neighbours. Whenever such support, for whatever reason, is not available to us, we can find ourselves feeling particularly negative or questioning the purpose of our life. Sometimes, this can lead to thoughts of suicide – a subject looked at in more detail in the chapter *Choose Life*.

What is important to recognise is the complex inter-relationship between the situations in which we find ourselves, the events that happen in our lives, and our thoughts and feelings. We can help ourselves, in the way of the prayer that asks:

God grant me the serenity to accept the things I cannot change, courage to change the things I can and wisdom to know the difference.[20]

But we can only help ourselves *so far*: we are made to be inter-dependent, and we benefit not only from sharing our troubles, but also by sharing the resources we each have to deal with them. Sometimes all we need is the chance to tell our story; to express our feelings and say how things really are. At other times, we may need advice or practical help. And in some situations – such as when we are made homeless or become ill or unemployed – we need to access appropriate local or national health or social services.

We also need to remember that experiencing positive mental health and well-being should not be equated with a life of unending happiness and enjoyment. To feel disappointed when a promised treat has to be cancelled, or to experience a sense of loss when our children leave home is both appropriate and healthy. Steve Hothersall reminds his student readers that:

it is mentally healthy to be sad when someone we love dies[21]

Being mentally healthy, and enjoying a sense of well-being, includes being able to express emotions appropriate to the circumstances we experience. Recognising this brings us back to the question asked in this chapter: half way to *where?*

While it is reasonable, when feeling lonely or depressed, or when life is seeming particularly difficult, to say to ourselves, 'if only I could feel happy', such ambition alone is unlikely to bring satisfaction. If happiness and enjoyment is all that want from life, however, we are likely either to face disappointment when we do not achieve it, or boredom and a lack of purpose to our life if we do.

The question, *'half way to where?'*, challenges us to reflect on the meaning and purpose of life, and to look for ways that will lead to well-being, not just for ourselves, but for those

20 Prayer known as the Serenity Prayer: see https://www.justpray.uk/serenity-prayer-a-full-look-at-its-origin-and-meaning (accessed 17/8/2020).

21 Hothersall, Steve *et al.*, *Social work and mental health in Scotland*, Exeter: Learning Matters Ltd., 2008, p. 6.

who travel with us on life's journey. Our search for well-being requires that we have concern for others as well as ourselves. At an event in Inverurie to celebrate Breathing Space Day [https://breathingspace.scot], on the first of February 2009, Mental Health Promotion worker, David Alexander, reminded us of this as he pointed out that the first two letters of the word 'well-being' are 'w' and 'e'.[22] If well-being is to be experienced, we must think about 'we', not merely about 'I'.

Desmond Tutu expresses this in a different way, as he describes the African concept 'ubuntu':

> *Ubuntu* is the essence of being human. It speaks of how my humanity is caught up and bound up inextricably with yours. It says, not as Descartes did, 'I think, therefore I am' but rather, 'I am because I belong'. I need other human beings in order to be human . . . I can be me only if you are fully you. I am because we are, for we are made for togetherness, for family. We are made for complementarity. We are created for a delicate network of relationships, of interdependence with our fellow human beings, with the rest of creation.[23]

This is what, as Christians, we believe is the message of Jesus when he talks of coming to bring us life 'its all its fullness'. Such fullness of life is intended, not just for some, but for all. Jesus came to bring light to all people in the world, by teaching how to so live lives of justice and love that everyone might know themselves loved and accepted – by God and by their neighbour.

Well-being and fullness of life

As stated earlier in this reflection, whoever we are and wherever we live, we are a part of our local community. People can choose to ignore this reality. And we ourselves can decide to withdraw and refuse to become involved in any community activity. But the realty is that just by *being there* we *are* a part of the community in which we live.

22   Comment made by David Alexander, Mental Health Promotion Aberdeen, on Breathing Space Day, 1 Feb 2009.

23   Tutu, Desmond, *God is not a Christian: speaking truth in times of crisis,* London: Ebury Publishing, 2013, p. 22.

In the past, when those who experienced the problems of mental illness were housed in huge asylums, built 'around the bend' with the intention that they might be forgotten or ignored, they were still *there*, and their presence had an impact on the community as a whole. Local residents were employed there; produce grown on their farms was sold in local shops. An interdependent relationship existed.

Living in a 'half way home' is not about living *outside* the local community. The half way home described in the story at the beginning of this chapter was built quite deliberately in a residential neighbourhood. This was done not only to indicate clearly its status – not as an institution, but as a *home* – but also to help residents to do all the usual activities of daily living, such as going to the local shops or having a meal out at a nearby café.

It is not where we live that includes or excludes us from the life of the community, but how we are perceived. Other people may treat us in ways that prevent us from sharing fully in the life of our community. And we ourselves may live with such feelings of worthlessness, or such lack of self-respect that, believing we are unacceptable, we distance ourselves from local community life.

As Christians, we believe that 'all are welcome in this place'.[24] This is true whether that 'place' is church, community, nation or world. We are, therefore, required to:

- ensure that *our* attitude is one of welcome and acceptance
- help those who feel isolated or rejected to recognise their own value and self-worth
- do all we can to gently but firmly challenge attitudes that threaten to devalue or exclude the other

Awareness of the need to ensure that everyone not only *is,* but actually *feels,* included in the life of our community is essential. A policy of inclusion can only do so much. It is love for our neighbour that makes belonging real in the lives of each individual.

Earlier in this reflection, we asked whether it is possible to experience well-being, while living with a diagnosis of mental illness. Although nobody can ever answer that question for anyone

---

24 *Church Hymnary*, Fourth edition, Norwich: Canterbury Press, 2005. Hymn no. 198. Words by Marty Haugen.

else, it seems – from all we have reflected on here – that it is, indeed possible to feel a sense of well-being in our life while also coping with the difficulties that mental illness can bring. Stories written by people experiencing mental illness, and published by the Scottish Recovery Network,[25] tell of this hope. Acceptance – accepting ourselves and accepting others – can transform life, bringing renewed sense of meaning and purpose.

Well-being, though, cannot be experienced in isolation. As humans, we are made to be inter-dependent. We need each other. Human relationships are essential to our well-being. Thinking about this from the perspective of our faith, we are aware, also, of the significance of our relationship with God to our well-being.

Welcome and acceptance; love and care; being valued simply because we are there: all these transform the lives of individuals and of communities. We *can* create communities of well-being.

So: is the journey of life towards well-being, or to the fullness of life, promised by Jesus?

As Christians, we believe that life in *all* its fullness is not possible until *all* people, throughout the world, are loved and cared for, valued and respected. As we work to create communities of well-being, then, we do so, aware that this vision for the world is not yet reality.

But we trust, too, that by accepting one another, caring for each other and supporting one another, it is possible for everyone in our community to discover well-being. And we pray that, working to create well-being in our own communities, the whole world will, one day, celebrate the fullness of life that is God's promise to us all.

---

25 Scottish Recovery Network, *Journeys of recovery: stories of hope and recovery from long term mental health problems,* Scottish Recovery Network, 2006.

Chapter Six
Choose Life

Story

Mandy and her daughter Natalie have been living together in their small flat since just after Natalie's birth nearly nine years ago. For the past two years, Mandy's partner John has also been living there. John's work frequently takes him away from home for a several days at a time, but Mandy describes him as a 'home bird at heart' when she talks about him. She tells me that he is happy to help around the house, and that he rarely shows any interest in going out in the evenings. Having him around is especially good for Natalie, Mandy goes on. Until John moved in, she had often seemed very withdrawn, spending almost all her time either with Mandy, or with her Nana, Mandy's mother, who lives close by. Now, however, she chats about her school friends, and has been to a few parties and also on several 'sleepovers' at her best friend's house. Natalie is clearly fond of John, and, Mandy tells me, has begun referring to him as 'Dad'.

Mandy says all this to me when we meet alone together for the first time. She has been coming to the centre run by a local mental health charity for several weeks now, but this is the first time she has asked to talk with me. She tells me that she had agreed to attend the group here twice a week 'to keep my doctor happy'. She had been to see her GP, she explains, because she felt like she just could not keep on struggling to cope. But, having made the effort to attend the appointment she had made, she was feeling so much better that she had been unable to say much, except that life seemed pretty hard right now. 'Typical, isn't it?' she commented. 'Just like toothache. You put up with it for ages, then when you finally pluck up the courage to go to the dentist it suddenly stops hurting.'

'What about just now?' I ask her. 'How do you feel today; now you've decided to tell me about it?' 'A bit the same', she replies: 'somehow when I'm *with* someone, it doesn't seem so bad'. 'Tell me about 'it' anyway,' I say to her.

Now that she has the opportunity to talk, Mandy struggles to know where to start. 'Just tell me a bit about yourself', I suggest. She begins to talk about Natalie and about John. Sensing her anxiety, as she tells me how her daughter has started to refer to her boyfriend as 'Dad', I ask how she is feeling right now. She turns away from me and puts her head in her hands.

Suddenly, after a moment or two, her mood seems to change again. She looks at me with a hesitant smile. 'I haven't told you about myself', she says, and goes on to tell me about the time when she was still a teenager, and had attempted to kill herself. She had been found in the school toilets by a class-mate, bleeding badly from the cuts she had made in both her wrists, and had been taken to hospital for attention. From there, she had been transferred to a children's mental health unit, but had pleaded to be discharged because, as she puts it 'they're all only kids in there'. Her Mum had taken her home and looked after her with the support of the friendly practice nurse and a counsellor. But Mandy never went back to school.

I am aware that Mandy is finding it easier to tell me about this painful experience from the past than to express how she is feeling about the present. Since she has just mentioned that it was her Mum who helped her through that time, I ask about her relationship with her mother today. Once again, she turns her head away.

It seems that at least part of Mandy's current anxiety has something to do with the relationships she has mentioned. But, right now, my priority is not to talk about these, but to focus on her feelings. She is distressed, and she has spoken of a previous suicide attempt. 'Are you telling me this because you feel like killing yourself now?' I gently ask her. She turns to face me and looks me squarely in the eye. 'You really understand that life can feel that bad?' she asks me. I nod, keeping eye contact with her. After what feels like an age, she reaches out and touches my hand. 'Thanks', she says, 'but, no, it's not *that* bad. It's just so bloody painful. And every time I think I've got it all worked out, it all goes wrong again'.

I tell her how glad I am that she is not feeling suicidal today, but also give her my telephone number and make her promise that she will contact me, or her GP, or tell someone here at the centre if she ever has thoughts of killing herself.

Having made this promise, Mandy asks if she can go. 'I can't think any more', she says, 'and anyway, I have to pick Nat up from school.' We agree to talk again later that week when she is next at the centre, and I suggest that we meet just after lunch, to allow more time together.

At our next meeting, I discover more about Mandy and her relationships. John's reliability, which had so attracted her to him a few years earlier, she now describes as 'boring'. 'He never wants to do anything,' she complains. 'He actually seems to enjoy those stupid games Nat's always wanting us to play.' Finding John's company boring, Mandy has started a relationship with a young man she met at the checkout at the supermarket where she works three evenings each week. 'John's happy to mind Nat,' she tells me, 'so I've said that my hours have been changed – they need me to help stock shelves after closing time – and he's daft enough to believe me. So me and Dave go for a drink instead'.

'Is that all you and Dave get up to?' I ask her. After a long silence, she responds to my question with one of her own. 'You go to church, I suppose, don't you?' I explain that in my work as chaplain, I lead worship in various parts of the hospital each Sunday and tell her, 'yes, I am a Christian'. 'You won't like my answer, then,' she goes on. 'But I'm going to tell you anyway. Just don't you tell me it's all wrong, and God will punish me, and all that crap, because I don't believe any of it. And anyhow Dave and I love each other and I want to be with him. It isn't wrong to be with the man you love, is it?'

I hear a lot more about Dave. About how exciting it is to be with him. Nothing about Dave is boring! Not like poor John who is at home with her daughter, and so proud that Natalie is beginning to trust him, and accept him as part of the family.

Dave doesn't know about John: Mandy has told him that her Mum looks after Natalie when she is out with him. Her Mum doesn't know about Dave: Mandy has asked John not to let on about the 'extra hours stacking shelves'. 'I'll surprise her with a big gift at Christmas' is how she has explained this secrecy to John. And John, of course, doesn't know about Dave.

Reflection

How can Mandy find an escape from her anxiety? What will enable her to experience a sense of well-being?

She is convinced, from her limited knowledge of Christian beliefs, that I will be critical of her present situation. In this, she is both right and wrong. She is wrong in her assumption that I will condemn her as a person; but right in her assumption that I will challenge the way she is treating her friends. She is wrong in thinking that I consider her distress as a punishment by God for her behaviour; but right to assume that I see a link between her present way of life and the anxiety she is experiencing.

From our perspective of concern for Mandy's well-being, as well as that of her young daughter Natalie, it would be all too easy for us to advise her to forget all about Dave, and to be thankful for the steadiness and reliability offered through her relationship with John. Pastoral care, however, is not about offering advice: it is, rather, about enabling people to discover for themselves the appropriate way forward. One of Mandy's difficulties, we can see, is that she is blaming others for her present situation. We will not help her at all, then, by offering advice, for this will merely give her the opportunity to blame us when things do not work out as she wants. Advice will not help Mandy on the journey towards well-being.

Mandy longs for excitement, and as she talks, we get a sense of how angry she was, just after the birth of her daughter, when her mother made it clear to her that 'now you are a mother there will be no more staying out all night'. Her mother's view, Mandy tells us, is this: 'if you are old enough to get pregnant, you are old enough to take care of the baby'. In other words, Mandy has been expected to face the consequences of her actions. But this is something Mandy is still finding herself unable to do.

Responsibility – not blame

She wants. So why can't she have? That is Mandy's struggle, and a major source of her anxiety. As she talks, we hear this tension between her sense of responsibility to her daughter and her resistance to her mother's expectations around this. We hear, in the way she describes her relationship with John, how she appreciates his reliability, even while she expresses her anger at how 'boring' being at home with him has become. And, as she talks about Dave, alongside her description of how thrilling it is to be out with him, we also pick up from her tone a sense of guilt about what she is doing.

She is, however, ready to blame everyone else rather than accept responsibility herself. If her mother had babysat for her more often when Natalie was younger, she would have got 'going out on the town' out of her system long ago. If John wasn't so boring then she would never have gone out with Dave. And Dave, according to her point of view, had persuaded her to continue meeting, even when she had wanted to say 'no'.

Mandy is by no means unusual in this. The cry of 'he – or she – started it!', heard so often by parents dealing with their children's arguments, goes on throughout life. We complain to friends about bad-tempered shop assistants or impatient bus drivers, and forget that we ourselves have been irritable at having to wait in a long queue or have been the cause of the delay by having no change for our fare.

Blaming others when things go wrong in our lives is a common reaction. Mostly, however, when we stop to reflect, we become aware of the part we ourselves have played in events. Excessive blaming of others is both unhelpful and unhealthy. We understand how, in the heat of the moment, it is all too easy to deny personal responsibility, but we recognise too, once the situation has 'died down', that we need to look again and see where our own words, or our own actions, have contributed to the difficulty.

The other extreme – excessive self-blame – is also unhealthy. Believing oneself to be at fault in all situations may be a sign of mental illness, just as complete inability to accept responsibility can be. These extreme positions are rare, and the people struggling to live with such painful feelings of *complete* denial or of *total* responsibility need specialist care and support.

To talk of 'blame' is rarely helpful. The word itself – whether or not the intention is to criticise or condemn – contains within it an element of judgement, which in turn creates feelings of guilt. Where the law has been broken, the terms 'blame' and 'guilt' have particular significance and, therefore, are appropriate to use. Here, however, we are concerned about helping each other on the journey of life. Blaming others and making them feel guilty will neither help them nor do much to resolve the situation. Equally, when someone has hurt or offended us, our 'no, no it wasn't *your* fault' is unhelpful, for our words deny that person the opportunity to accept responsibility or to apologise.

Honest recognition of responsibility is important to creating and maintaining healthy relationships. In caring relationships, we help one another – often by sensitive teasing or a gentle reprimand – to keep a healthy balance between denying all responsibility and believing ourselves completely responsible, whether for things that go wrong or for those that work out well. We remind each other, too, to be realistic and objective: sometimes the unexpected just happens!

Personal responsibility

So how might we help Mandy? She believes that she has the 'right' to enjoy life. But, by trying to get what she wants, she is not taking responsibility for how her behaviour is affecting the people around her. It is not that she is unaware of their feelings: she senses that John is suspicious about her new late evening work, and she admits to feeling guilty every time she hears Natalie refer to John as her 'Dad'. And when asked about her mother, she replies: 'Mum hasn't said anything yet. But she's sensed since I was a kid if I'd done something I shouldn't.'

Mandy seems unable to take responsibility for her actions. She cannot make the connection between what she is *doing* and what she and others are *feeling*. This may be because of past painful experiences in her own life: her suicide attempt as a teenager is a sign that this may be the case.

Mandy's focus on herself and what she *wants* may, however, also reflect the values of the society in which she has grown up. She has been brought up in a culture that focuses on the rights of the individual. In present day western society, we are encouraged to see personal happiness is the ultimate goal. Each person is taught to know their rights as an *individual*, and to believe that the only responsibility we need have is to seek that happiness for ourselves. If other people don't do the same, that is *their* problem, not *ours*.

If we were to accept this view of life, then the help we would offer to Mandy would most likely be in the form of a pill to blank out her feelings of anxiety and block out any rumblings of guilt. By removing her 'symptoms', we could leave her free to do as she pleases.

But we know that this is no real solution to Mandy's problem. Why? Because we recognise that, were we to 'help' Mandy in this way, we are doing nothing at all to make life more bearable for the others in the story. That is not all. We are also aware that, by letting Mandy continue to tell herself that the search for happiness and the desire for instant satisfaction is all there is to life, we are denying her the possibility of ever finding the 'life in all its fullness' that we believe is available to us all.

Pastoral care should always be non-judgemental. But this does not mean that it never challenges. Or that it never has the expectation that people can change. Accepting people just as they are is a crucial aspect of pastoral care. But if *all* we do is accept, and we never challenge or expect more from those for whom we care, we are, in fact, treating them as less human than we believe ourselves to be.

As Christians, we recognise that life is a journey: a road along which we discover meaning and purpose as we learn and grow. To deny this possibility to others is to deny their humanity. To assume that an individual *cannot* change and grow, or that the attitudes and assumptions held by any society are fixed and unalterable, is to deny that significance of the resurrection. As Christian Aid's 'strap-line' puts it: 'we believe in life before death'. The fullness of life that we seek; the community well-being that we work to create – these are promised to us now. Our Christian hope is not merely for a distant tomorrow. It is for new life *now*: 'on earth as it is in heaven'.

If Mandy is to be helped to grow, and to find genuine happiness in life – and not just instant pleasure – then we will have to challenge her to take responsibility for the effect her behaviour is having on her own well-being as well as that of the people around her. She will need encouragement to look at her situation from *their* perspective, and support as she considers what might be best for them as well as for herself.

Responsibility and relationship with God

Mandy makes it clear that she has no time for religion. Her suspicion of me, when she first discovers that I am a Christian, is based on a jumble of assumptions she has about God. As a young child, she had sometimes stayed overnight with her grandmother, who had read to her stories such as 'Noah and the Ark' and 'David and Goliath'. These, she now explains to me, 'put me off God': she sees God as destroying people who do not obey him and encouraging those who believe in him to kill those who don't. Understandably, from this perspective, she has not been interested in developing a relationship with such a God. She has been inside a church once recently, for the funeral of a school friend's baby. But that experience only confirmed her views about God. 'We were told that he was so precious that God needed him up in heaven', she told me angrily. 'If only God knew how upset poor Kate is now. How could he have taken him from her like that?'

It is not surprising, when we hear all this, that Mandy has no interest in God. Where Bible stories are told out of context, and with no attempts at explanation or clarification, it is all too easy for them to be misunderstood. When we do not stop and think before making comments, or when we assume that ideas that we ourselves have found comforting will bring comfort to *others,* we risk hurting the people we are trying to help. Not only that, but our lack of reflection and sensitivity to their need can result in their turning further from God.

Believing that God's love is for everyone, we want others to discover for themselves the help and sense of purpose on life that relationship with God can bring. Each one of us, therefore, has the responsibility to ensure that what we do and say in our pastoral care enables that love to be discovered and enjoyed by all others as well as ourselves.

As Christians, we believe that God loves *unconditionally.* There is *nothing* that anyone must – or indeed can – do to 'earn' God's love: God loves because God is love. But we can see how a brief look at the Bible can appear to tell us something very different.

'*If* you obey the words of the Lord your God', we read in Deuteronomy chapter 30. '*If* you obey . . . then God will bless you.' Conditional. Or is it? We can certainly understand how Mandy would see it that way. And in much of its history the church has chosen to interpret it like that: 'if you believe in God, you will prosper' has been a persuasive method to achieve conversions, as has 'if you reject God, he will punish you with pain or sickness'. Even today, such views are expressed, though maybe not in these words. Telling people that they are not 'worthy' to receive communion, however, is saying much the same thing. As is implying that it is lack of faith, and not the horrendous circumstances being coped with, that is the root cause of anyone's anxiety or depression.

The message contained in this 'if' is not that we are being threatened by God; forced into a certain lifestyle in order to earn His blessing. The message is, rather, one of encouragement to live *well*. We read in verse 19 of Deuteronomy chapter 30 that we must choose between life and death; choose between experiencing life as full of meaning and hope, or life as mere survival.

It is clear that the *choice is ours*. God's *hope* is that we 'choose life'. God wants to help *all* people on the journey of life. God's plan is that we *all* live *well*: that we do not merely survive, but thrive, as we seek the life in all its fullness that is his promise for all people.

If, however, we choose to reject the God who created us, then there will be consequences. We must take responsibility for the choices we make. The Bible puts it in stark terms: the choice we make is a matter of life and death. Strong language is used to make the point clear. If we choose God's way of love and try to welcome and accept each other in the way we would like others to accept us . . . If we choose God's way of peace and learn to live in harmony with the people around us, even when we find it hard to understand them or even to like them . . . If we live this way, then we will have good relationships with one another and receive the care and support that we all need on the journey of life.

If, on the other hand, we turn from God's way and try to 'do our own thing', we may, as the Prodigal Son did, discover short-term happiness. But selfishness, and lack of concern for the people around us, will bring problems and difficulties. Why should others help us in our time of need, if we have refused to help them or told them that their struggles were caused by their own thoughtless actions?

Turning from God will not literally kill us, but it will lead us on a different path than the one that leads to the fullness of life that God promises. As a twentieth century hymn writer, Fred Kaan puts it:

All that kills abundant living,
  let it from the earth be banned;[26]

---

26 *Church Hymnary*, Fourth edition, Norwich: Canterbury Press, 2005. Hymn number 706. Words by Fred Kaan.

Kaan's plea is for the healing of relationships; healing between nations as well as the healing of individual relationships broken by selfishness, thoughtlessness and rejection of the reality of our human inter-dependence. In verse 1 of this hymn, he invites us to sing:

> For the healing of the nations,
> Lord, we pray with one accord;
> for a just and equal sharing
> of the things that earth affords.
> To a life of love in action
> help us rise and pledge our word.

Individual actions have consequences in the community around us. Mandy needs to see how her own desire for happiness and excitement in life is affecting the people around her. Her 'right' to do what she wants is having an impact on Natalie's 'right' to a secure and stable upbringing. Her 'right' to enjoy life is denying both John and Dave the 'right' to a relationship with her that is based on love and trust. 'Choose life', for Mandy, means finding the freedom to enjoy life *through*, not despite, the honesty and integrity necessary within loving relationships.

Choosing life, in this sense of accepting the responsibilities implicit in inter-dependent relationships, will enrich life not only for Mandy herself, but for Dave, John and Natalie. By helping Mandy to look beyond the here and now, as well as by enabling her to understand the way her behaviour has an effect upon her feelings, we can encourage Mandy to begin to live *well*: to travel the road that leads to well-being.

God's hope for us: 'choose life'

'Choose life' is what God wants us to do. To choose the way that leads to well-being. Life is good: that is the message of the creation stories in the book of Genesis. To be more precise, it is *inter-dependent life* that is good. All of creation is inter-dependent. *Relationships* are crucial to the way of life that our God asks us to choose.

Choosing life means choosing to live our lives in relationship with others. It is as we let ourselves be cared for, and as we learn how to care both *about* and *for* our neighbour, that we discover well-being.

Building healthy and life-enhancing relationships takes time and effort. We know this to be so as we puzzle over what humanity now needs to do if the resources of our planet are to be preserved; resources on which all living creatures depend. We know this to be so, also, in all our personal relationships: as we struggle, for example, to keep our temper when our mother-in-law with dementia asks us for the fifth time in so many minutes when her husband, dead for many years, will be home from work. Maintaining good relationships is also hard work. Scottish theologian Donald Baillie, quoting the wise words of a much earlier writer, Baron von Hugel, expresses the effort required with these words:

> I kiss my child not only because I love it: I kiss it also in order to love it.[27]

It is because love is *not* easy that God came to us in human form. By following the example of Jesus, we learn how to love and care for each other.

Our hope for each other: 'choose life'

Encouraging each other to choose the way that leads to well-being, and supporting one another through times of struggle and difficulty, is what the pastoral care of the church is about. All of us need help; some more than others. Most of us find ourselves especially appreciative of friendship and support during periods of stress or uncertainty or illness.

There may come a time in any of our lives when such help and support can mean the difference between life and death. Facing the difficulties of life alone, not knowing what to do or where to turn for help, can lead anyone to think about suicide as a way of putting an end to their distress. Discovering that someone cares can bring a glimmer of light into the darkness of despair. There may be no easy way through the difficulties currently being experienced, but such a glimmer can be enough to help us through an immediate crisis. In the depths of such extreme suffering, having someone beside us – alongside us in our pain – can give us the courage, literally, to turn from death to life.

Preventing death by suicide, however, is not only about doing what we can to stop someone from killing herself, or himself, in a moment of crisis. Helping one another to 'choose life' is part of the

27   Baillie, Donald M., *The theology of the sacraments and other papers*, London: Faber and Faber Ltd., 1957, p. 54.

on-going work of any caring community. For it is, as we do what we can to create communities of well-being, that we encourage one another to turn from ways that lead to suffering, and to discover the pathway on which life can be lived *well*.

Suicide prevention

Most of us will admit to feeling 'out of our depth' when we first think about suicide, wondering what on earth we could do – or say – that would help a friend or colleague in such distress. Although a natural reaction, we will not discover ways of helping if we refuse to think about suicide or to deny the reality of suicidal thoughts. Scotland has a worryingly high suicide rate. As people seeking to improve well-being in our local communities, it is important to look at the issue of suicide and become involved in suicide prevention.

The Scottish Government's Action Plan for suicide prevention[28] outlines work that is going on across the country to reduce the suicide rate and to provide help and support for people feeling suicidal.

Suicide prevention, however, is also about ensuring that people can access care and support before any difficulties become crises that cannot be coped with. Developing caring communities is an important aspect of suicide prevention. Recognising this, a public awareness campaign, launched on World Suicide Prevention Day, 10th September, 2020, provides easy-to-access information about sources of support and ways of caring.[29] Thoughts and suggestions about how to care for a friend who is having thoughts of suicide can be found in an excellent short cartoon-style video called '*Ask, tell – save a life: every life matters*'.[30]

The local church may well be a place where someone feeling suicidal turns for help. A neighbour or friend in distress may knock at your door. Some basic guidelines for suicide prevention are mentioned here: more information, advice and details of training courses, can be found on the websites listed at the end of this chapter.

Where you have concern for the immediate safety of a person, it is *essential* that he or she is not left alone, and that emergency

28 https://www.gov.scot/publications/scotlands-suicide-prevention-action-plan-life-matters (accessed 27 August 2020).

29 www.unitedtopreventsuicide.co.uk (website live from 10th September 2020).

30 https://vimeo.com/338176393 (accessed 27 August 2020).

help is sought by calling 999. By being there with the person, and listening to whatever they want to talk about, you are – at the very least – keeping them alive until specialist help arrives. It is likely, however, that you will be doing far more than this. Knowing that somebody cares can ease pain and give back that glimmer of hope which may have gone out of their life.

It is also important to 'ask the suicide question'. A common misunderstanding is that asking a person if they are feeling suicidal will put the idea into their head. This, however, is not so. All evidence indicates that, by having the confidence to ask, 'have you thought about killing yourself?', you might well be helping to save that person's life.

Imagine feeling so desperate that you cannot believe that anyone could understand just how awful you are feeling. Your mind is whirling, and your thoughts and feelings are all confused. You want to tell the person there with you that you just can't face life any more, but fear that the intensity of your pain will drive them away. Or you sense that they will not understand that your life could really be that bad. So you walk away, with your pain.

Now imagine the sense of relief that you feel, when, instead, that person asks you if you feel so awful that you have thought about killing yourself. There! The words have been said! This person is trying to understand. This person is willing to listen. This person will not be destroyed by your distress. *Now* you can talk more freely.

If we can find the courage to ask this most difficult of questions we will, just by doing so, have helped the person in distress. By asking about suicidal thoughts, we are showing that it is okay to talk about them. We are indicating that we are prepared to listen to the painful things that need to be talked about.

Any death by suicide is a tragedy that any caring community should do its utmost to prevent. Sometimes, the level of distress a person is experiencing goes unnoticed until it is too late. All of us need to become more aware of factors in our own lives and in the lives of others that can lead to us having thoughts that life is not worth living or that hope has gone.

Living in a remote or isolated area, for example, has been identified as a risk factor. While this does not, of course, mean that all of us who live in such areas will have thoughts of suicide, this knowledge highlights the importance of friendship and of supportive relationships. Being alone in an isolated landscape, for example, does not *of itself* make us feel suicidal. Indeed, the opposite can be true, as we renew our inner strength or take the time we need to resolve complex issues while walking through woodland or climbing hillsides. *Combined with other factors,* however, such as threat of unemployment, marriage breakdown, low self-esteem, or loss of a sense of meaning and purpose for our life, being isolated and alone can lead us to thoughts of suicide.

Another aspect of life in Scotland that puts many of us at risk of suicide is the Scots character that in so many other ways we are right to be proud of. Our ability to keep going in difficult circumstances is what has seen our nation through so many difficult periods of history. Crofters evicted during the time of the Clearances made new lives for themselves in Canada and other parts of the world. Islanders in more recent times have stood up against the power of absentee landlords. But the image many of us have of ourselves as invincible Scots may also be our downfall. A report on the health of our nation sums up this tension in its title, *The Scots may be brave but they are neither healthy nor happy.*[31]

It is hard to talk about problems in a culture that values the 'stiff upper lip' and almost impossible for boys and young men, brought up to believe that 'real men don't cry', to find ways to express the feelings of distress or anguish that are common to us all.

A sad reflection of our present-day western society is that, for many of us – not only for men – it can be easier and more acceptable to ask for help from an anonymous stranger than from family or friend. Although it is important to recognise that, for some people in distress, seeking help from a stranger is clearly beneficial, it is also true that many of us feel best supported and cared for by those closest to us. The most appropriate response, on first noticing that a friend or neighbour appears withdrawn or 'out of sorts' is, therefore, not to immediately suggest that they call a help-line or seek professional help. That may be a useful, or even a necessary next step, so it is helpful to be aware of contacts and telephone numbers.[32]

---

31 Bell, David and Blanchflower, David, University of Stirling, *The Scots may be brave but they are neither healthy nor happy,* Scotecon, 2004.

32 Support in Mind Scotland: https://www.supportinmindscotland.org. uk. Breathing Space: https://breathingspace.scot. Samaritans: https://www. samaritans.org.

An invitation to sit down with a cup of tea and to 'tell me about it', however, is often enough to relieve the pressure and encourage the one in difficulty to open up about their feelings.

Suicide prevention, however, as said above, is not only about preventing an individual from acting on their suicidal thoughts. It is also about ensuring that life never feels so bad that death seems the only solution. As Christians, we aim to provide pastoral care and support to help people through times of particular difficulty. But we are also committed to doing what we can to prevent problems and difficulties arising in the first place. 'Let justice flow like a stream, and righteousness like a river that never goes dry' is what God asks of us in Amos 5.24.

This image presents water as enriching and life-giving. As we know only too well, however, now that our country is experiencing an increase of heavy rainfall and the resultant flooding, water can also be frightening and dangerous.

In the ASIST – Applied Suicide Intervention Skills Training – programme,[33] the risk of suicide is portrayed as a river flowing through our lives. When life is going well and we have few problems, or there are plenty resources and support to help us to deal with them, the river may appear pleasant and non-threatening. Experiencing pain or loss, however, might pull us into deeper water, where we are at risk of drowning. If we cry out for help, our friends can pull us into shallower water again. Without such friends, though, turning to alcohol or drugs may drag us once more into the faster flowing water. Or we may shut out all contact with others and become more and more isolated and depressed. Pulled along by the force of the river, further difficulties may push us over the edge – as the water tumbles down a waterfall.

This 'river of suicide' has tributaries that flow into it. 'Up river' from our present experience are all the events that have helped shape who we are. These tributaries contribute to how we cope with life. Childhood experiences, for example, will make us more, or less, likely to seek help when life gets tough. Recent setbacks, perhaps minor or apparently insignificant at the time, will, in times of anxiety, contribute to feelings of despair or arouse feelings of hopelessness.

33 Details of this and other training courses can be found at: http://www. healthscotland.scot/health-topics/suicide (accessed 27 Aug. 2020).

Past events in our lives, painful memories, or lack of care and support, can all act as 'contributaries' to suicidal thinking or action.

Suicide prevention is as much about doing what we can to remove such 'contributaries', or to reduce their harmful effects, as about rescuing people from the life-threatening rapids.

The journey to well-being

Life is for living *well*. All of us would want to travel the journey of life without suffering or pain. We know that this is unrealistic. But we know, too, that by helping one another, such pain and suffering can be made bearable. Care and support enriches the life of both the one who gives the care and the one who receives it.

Working for justice – ensuring that our communities are places where everyone feels welcome, valued and respected – helps us on the journey to well-being. Loving our neighbour – caring in times of need – helps us on the journey to well-being.

God asks us to 'choose life'. The fullness of life promised to us can begin to be found as we choose the way God has created for us: the way of inter-dependent relationship. We need each other, and it is through relationship with one another that we will find the meaning and purpose in life that gives us hope for both now and the future. And we need God's guidance if we are to turn from the selfishness and greed that leads to immediate gratification and short-lived happiness.

The well-being that God promises is to be discovered *now*, though not yet to be experienced in *all* its fullness. God's Kingdom has yet to come in all its glory. But, with the birth of Jesus, the Kingdom has begun. God's Kingdom on earth, here and now, where God's love, God's peace and God's hope can be enjoyed and celebrated by all peoples of the world.

These God-given gifts are found as we care for, and about, each other on the journey of life. 'Choosing life' means this: that we, as the prophet Micah reminds us, 'do what is just, show constant love and live in humble fellowship with our God' (Micah 6.8). Choosing to live this way, we play our part in the development of communities of well-being: places in which love can, indeed, be shared, and in which peace can be enjoyed and hope discovered.

Chapter Seven

Only One Magpie

Story

It is early afternoon and I am visiting people in one of the acute psychiatric wards. As usual, I go first to the nurses' office to check that now is a convenient time to visit. One of the nurses asks if I could knock on Andy's door and see if he would like to talk. He has been unusually quiet, and the nurses are concerned. Do I have time to sit with him, and perhaps encourage him to say what is troubling him?

I knock at the door and his room-mate answers. I know Iain well, and he smiles when he sees me. 'Not looking for me just now, I hope', he says. 'I'm just off to the gardening project. But could you come and see how our beans are doing later on?' I tell him that I would like to come, but cannot promise that I will have the time today. 'Fair enough', Iain replies. 'See you if I see you, then. I'll be there until five.'

I knock again and introduce myself to Andy, who is leaning on his pillows and staring out of the window. 'Okay if I sit down for a bit?' I ask. 'Suit yourself', says, without looking round. 'I expect my key nurse sent you.' 'You're right', I admit, 'but I was planning to say 'hi' to you anyway. You weren't here when I was in last week.'

Andy continues to gaze out of the window. 'Dull day', he reports, 'look at those dark clouds'. 'Dull outside', I reply. 'Is it dull inside too?' Andy is quiet for a long time, then he turns to face me. 'Boring', he tells me. 'Nothing to do. Not that I *feel* like doing anything . . .'

'What *do* you feel like right now?' I ask him. 'Really want to know?' is his cautious response. 'I really do', I assure him. 'I'd like to get to know you, and if I can help in any way, then I will try my best'.

A long silence follows. Then Andy turns once more to look out of the window. 'You know what I saw out there?' he says. 'A magpie. Just one. That's bad luck you know, seeing just one. Means something bad is going to happen. I'm really worried. I've seen it twice. What's going to happen to me?' [Andy is thinking of the superstition about magpies and the rhyme, 'One for sorrow, two for joy; three for a girl and four for a boy'].

I continue to sit with Andy, and we talk about his worries. I hear about his family, about their disappointment when he lost his job. He tells me how anxious he is about being in hospital, and how worried he is about how he will cope when he is discharged.

'And the magpie?' I eventually ask. 'seeing that bird out there is making it all feel worse?'

'Yes', he agrees. 'It's just outside my window. Like it's got a message just for me. You know that rhyme: 'one for sorrow, two for joy'? It's there, on its own. Something bad is going to happen. I just know it'.

I remind him of some of the difficulties he has described to me, and assure him that all the staff are here to help him. And then I gently suggest to him that the presence of a magpie cannot change his situation – neither for better nor for worse. 'But don't you know that rhyme?' he persists. 'They wouldn't write it for nothing, would they? They must believe that one bird on its own means bad luck'.

I decide that now is the time to share my perspective. 'You know what?' I say to Andy, 'that rhyme *is* talking about something bad happening. But it's not bad for *us*: it's bad for the magpie. Do you know that magpies mate for life? 'Two for joy' means they are together, ready to build their nest, and lay their eggs. Maybe that next bit of the rhyme about 'three for a girl and four for a boy' is something about the number of eggs they lay. Or maybe that bit is just to keep the rhyme going. But one for sorrow? Think about that poor magpie. Maybe he has lost his mate. Maybe she didn't survive the winter.'

Andy and I continue to sit together. We look at each other, both thinking hard. Andy breaks the silence. 'I see what you mean. Maybe it *is* the magpie that's unhappy. But even so, I've got a lot to deal with, haven't I?'

'You have indeed', I acknowledge. 'But you're not like that poor magpie. You are not alone. We're all here to help you. And you said your Mum is quite understanding, didn't you?'

Suddenly Andy looks tired. 'Enough thinking for one day?' I suggest. He nods. 'What shall I tell your key nurse?' I ask him.

Andy brightens. 'Tell him I *will* take him on at snooker', he says, with the hint of a smile. 'The table's in that room at the end of the corridor; sort of private. Good chance to tell him a bit how I'm feeling while we play.'

'Good chance indeed', I say as I get up to leave. 'I'll see you on Thursday if you're around. Okay?'

'Okay' he says, then looks down at his feet. 'Thanks', he mutters. As I walk back to the nurses' office, I say a whispered prayer: 'Thank you, God'.

Reflection

Here we have a story about Andy, who has a problem with a story about magpies. The story is creating problems for him because thinking about it is adding to the difficulties he is already having to face.

In this chapter, we think about the influence stories can have on us. We think about different types of stories. We look, first, at the story of our own life, and at how our own story can affect both how we perceive our problems and how we respond when others turn to us for help. We then think about the stories that we hear – those we are told or have read to us – and consider their influence.

When the stories that have become a part of our life are *helpful* to us when dealing with a difficult situation, developing a new relationship, or coming to terms with a new experience, we may hardly even notice their influence. Most of us, for most of the time, will not give much thought to how far our earliest experiences direct our day to day life and relationships. We may spend little time pondering whether the Bible stories, or folk tales, that we heard as a child are affecting the decisions we make today.

But when such stories clash with our present-day experience, we are likely to be more conscious of the influence they have on us. As we search for a way of coping with a particular difficulty, the story that comes into our mind may confuse us, or worry us, or – as was true for Andy – leave us feeling upset or anxious. When a story that we recall seems to be contributing to our present distress, then we may need guidance from others. It can be helpful to listen to how someone else interprets the same story, or to discover an alternative perspective on a story that is upsetting us.

Life stories and pastoral care

We now consider the stories we tell each other about our lives. When a friend, or colleague, comes to us for help or support, we ask them to 'say more about it' or to 'tell me what happened'. We listen to their story. We hear their own particular understanding – their perception – of what is causing their worry or concern. But, if people are to be helped, we need to encourage and enable them not just to *tell* their story, but also to begin to *respond to* it. As they *tell* of their experience, and *hear* it as a story, it becomes possible to reflect on the meaning of what has happened and to consider various ways of responding to – and finding ways of coping with – whatever has occurred.

It may also be appropriate, and helpful, to guide a person to see their situation from the point of view of another: to recognise how their own feelings may have influenced the way they now respond.

Your next-door neighbour, for example, calls in to talk to you about how upset he is feeling. He had come home yesterday from an unusually difficult meeting at work, and had hoped to be able to relax with a drink, and tell his wife all about it. She, however, as soon as he sat down, had put his meal down in front of him, and switched on the television. He had really needed her at that moment, he tells you, and is still feeling rejected and unloved.

You listen to his story of events the previous evening, acknowledging how hard it must have been for him. You want to help, and feel it would be beneficial for him to consider also how his wife may have been feeling. But you do not want to give him the impression that you believe him to be thoughtless or selfish. So you ask him to 'say a bit more about what happened last night'.

He tells you that he had got home about an hour after his usual time, and that he had opened the door and called out to his wife, 'I need a drink *now*, dear: it's been an awful day.' There is a pause, and you ask him to continue. 'Jean told me that supper was already ready', he goes on, 'but I felt too uptight to eat just then'. You think to yourself, 'what might he have been uptight about?', and 'how might Jean have been feeling?' So you let him talk a bit longer, and help him to express his emotions, and then you ask how he thinks his wife might have been feeling. His immediate reaction is anger. 'You on her side, then?' he challenges you. You explain that you are not on anybody's 'side', and remind him gently that in any relationship difficulty we need to be aware of how each one is feeling, if the difficulty is to be resolved. He calms down, and you comment that, when you had seen Jean going in and out the day before, she had seemed anxious and in a hurry. 'I didn't get in to see her', you go on, but 'I was wondering whether everything was okay'. 'That's strange', comments your neighbour. 'She told me at breakfast that she was going to spend the day preparing her talk for the Guild next week.' There is a long pause while you both think about what has been said, and about what it might mean. Then, suddenly, your neighbour says he is going, and climbs over the wall into his own garden.

Later that day, there is a knock at the door. Jean and her husband are both there. 'We're not coming in', they say. 'We just popped round to thank you for your help.' Having felt a bit useless earlier in the day, and somewhat dissatisfied with your attempt at helping after he had left so abruptly that morning, you are pleased, as well as surprised, to hear that they feel you have been helpful. 'My old aunt phoned just after lunch yesterday', Jean explains. 'She had fallen and was still feeling dizzy. So I went round to see her, and thought I had better phone the doctor. Then I came back for the car to take her round to the surgery, but I forgot my purse and had to come back so I could pay at the chemist for the bandage she recommended'. Her husband then continues their story: 'she then had to rush, as she wanted dinner to be on the table when I got in. She knew about that meeting I was worried about and wanted the meal to be all ready as soon as I arrived. *And* she'd hardly prepared anything for her talk. But then I spoiled it all by insisting on having a drink first'. 'We've sorted it all out now, though', adds Jean. 'So, thanks for reminding us that it always takes two – to make up, as well as to argue.'

This example is a reminder of the importance of hearing the *wider* story, and not just the immediate, or most distressing, aspects. There are, of course, dozens of other inter-connecting stories which will have had their influence on the way the particular story you have listened to unfolds. There is the story of the marriage relationship between Jean and her husband, and the story of their priorities. Which, for example, is more important to each of them – his paid employment commitments, or the voluntary work she is involved in at her local church? Is faith important in both their lives, or is it a cause of tension between them? Is her family, including her aged aunt, taking up more of her attention than her husband and his needs? Does he see work, and relationships with colleagues, as more important to him than family and friends? All these 'stories' will impact on the one particular part of the story of their relationship that they have invited you to share. And that wider story is, in turn, influenced by the story of the culture in which they now live, as well as of the communities in which they each lived, prior to their marriage to each other.

In our pastoral care, each story we hear will always be only a part of the life story of each individual. And each individual life story is told from within the context of the wider community and culture.

Looking at problems or difficulties in this way can help to identify which aspects may require a decision to be made, or a change in attitude or behaviour. Some situations require such action; others may be better dealt with by support from family and friends, or by seeking help from people skilled in dealing with that particular issue. Seeing the 'bigger picture' can also enable us to see whether a situation is one that must be accepted and coped with, or one that can be changed. It also helps us to consider whether or not a particular problem is one that raises issues of a social or political nature, and so may require a challenge to current local or national policies.

Put in a different way, this reflecting together on the meaning of 'my story of my problem' encourages us to look at it within the context of that prayer referred to earlier, in the chapter, *Halfway to Where?*:

> God, grant me the serenity to accept the things I cannot change, the courage to change the things I can, and the wisdom to know the difference.

By looking carefully together at the wider context of any story, we are helping the person with the problem to identify the specific *detail* of what can and cannot be done. Reflecting together in this way, we also declare our commitment to supporting that person. We are showing that we are not just interested in the story itself, but in the *meaning* of that story in her or his life. As we both *listen to* and *respond to* the stories we hear, we make it clear that we will remain alongside, while our friend, or our neighbour, finds a way of coping, or dealing with, the present situation.

In other words, we are rooting our belief that God is always present among us, in the emotional and practical support that we are giving to the one in need. In our pastoral care, we believe that God is with us, guiding our words and our actions, and we also trust that God is with the one in need. We believe, too, that, as 'Christ's Body' on earth, our presence is a sign of God's presence. We proclaim that God is love, not as 'theory' but as practical reality, through our listening and our caring.

Our *own* life story and pastoral care

We have been thinking about the stories people may share with us when they come to us for help or support. As we care for one another, however, it is important to recognise how our *own* stories affect our pastoral care.

Our *response* to the stories people share with us is influenced by:

- our present circumstances
- how we are feeling
- our past experiences
- the culture in which we grew up

Our pastoral care will be more helpful, where we recognise the influence of these factors. They affect the way we experience and respond to problems, and they also affect the way we care.

When asked to help, we may find ourselves focusing so much on *that particular person* and on *that particular problem* that we forget that our response will be influenced by our *own* life story. Our care is more effective when we acknowledge this. It is when we are aware of the influence personal experience can have on our pastoral care that we are able to 'step outside' of such influence and to care more appropriately.

Let us return to the example above, of our neighbour and his wife Jean. His story of what happened is affected both by how he was feeling the night before, when he arrived home from work, and by what he is feeling and thinking as he describes those events to you. His previous experiences, both with Jean, and with others, and how he remembers feeling and responding, will also influence the way his story unfolds. Culture too has its influence. National or community culture, or tradition, has a part to play, as do the cultures accepted as 'normal' by the families of both Jean and her husband. These cultures, in addition, may create conflicting responses. Husband and wife may both be young enough to have grown up in a national culture which no longer sees the role of the wife as waiting patiently for her man to return home, with her shoulder ready for crying on at the end of a hard day at work. Jean's upbringing may have reinforced this view in her, but the relationship between her husband's parents may have been one in which the role of wife as 'waiting at home to support' was reinforced rather than challenged.

As caring neighbour, though, you too will have your own feelings and expectations, and not only about the story that you are invited to respond to. When the doorbell rings, you walk to answer it, with thoughts in your head that may range from a curious 'I wonder who that might be?' to 'oh no, I was hoping for a quiet evening alone'. How you are feeling will play a part in how you respond to your neighbour and to his unfolding story.

Previous experience will also play its part in your response here as 'carer'. Your ongoing relationship with your neighbours will affect how you hear the story of recent events in their life, as will your relationships with other neighbours and friends.

If you have been used to family life, in which disagreements frequently occur, but are equally speedily resolved, you may feel relaxed when listening to a tale of tension between the husband and wife next door. But if your only experience of tension at home resulted in your parents' divorce, you may feel quite ill at ease when your neighbour opens up to you. All this will affect the way you respond when your help is requested.

Culture will affect your response to the story, just as it influenced your neighbour in its telling. Often – since family patterns and traditions are closely intertwined with the norms of community and national culture – there will be little or no tension between your view of the situation, and how it is perceived in the wider cultural context. Sometimes, however, the culture, or traditions, of the family and community you grew up in may differ considerably from the culture in which you live, and may be very different again from your neighbour's cultural context.

Such cultural differences can create difficulties in the search for a resolution to any problem. For example, your neighbour has felt able to come to you for help, so it would appear that, within his culture and his own experience of family life, it is acceptable to talk *outside* of the family about tensions *within* the family. But if you, however, come from a tradition in which talking of family problems to an outsider is so unacceptable as to be considered 'taboo', you might find it almost impossible to listen to your neighbour's story, far less feel able to respond to it, or to offer any help.

The situation would be very different, were it you who is the one who feels at ease with the sharing of family problems. Your neighbour could be the one in whose family life such sharing is normally 'taboo', but yet, for some reason not yet apparent, he is so distressed that he has overcome all inhibitions placed on him by both culture and family, and come to you, desperate for help. In such circumstances you will need to be prepared, both to hear and respond to his story, and to be sensitive to the cultural 'norm' that he has broken, in order to get the help he needs.

Who we are, and the various cultures within which we grow and develop, all have a significant part to play in the way in which we hear and respond to the stories told by the people around us.

The influence of stories we hear

The stories that we hear, or read, also influence the ways in which we think and act. Their influence is often most significant when we feel stressed, or under pressure, when we are unwell, or finding it difficult to know what decision to make.

The significance of stories – perhaps especially those that have entered our culture in the form of tales or folklore – is that they are heard and absorbed by most of us, almost unconsciously. Just as we accept the values and behaviours of the people we grow up around, before the influences of wider society may lead us to question or challenge them, so, too, do we the stories we hear affect us at a sub-conscious level.

If, when we were young, we were told stories about bravery, and how it is the strong who are successful, we may find it very hard to admit, as an adult, that we feel exhausted and defeated by the problems we are facing. But, if we grew up on stories about a whole range of characters, who experienced a wide variety of situations, and responded in many different ways, we are more likely to be aware of various possible responses to the situations we face.

As children, we hear in stories what we are ready, or able, to hear. The wonder of such folk and fairy tales it that they 'speak' to our children in different ways as they grow and develop.

A child who, on first hearing the story of Little Red Riding Hood, giggled with pleasure at the idea of a wolf lying in Grandma's bed, may suddenly begin to put her hands over her ears and refuse to listen, or may tell us that the story is 'too scary'. Apprehension about staring school, or the death of a grandparent, may be triggers to a new sensitivity to the 'scary' aspects contained within the tale mentioned above.

A child listening to a story involving a 'wicked' adult, such as the tale of Hansel and Gretel, or of Cinderella, will, depending on their own particular situation and their own individual feelings and personality, respond in his or her own unique way. One child may be reassured to hear that the children in the story also feel the hate or anger that he himself is feeling towards an adult in his own life; another – or the same child at a different stage of development – may feel frightened at discovering that some adults are not to be trusted.

As adults, it is important that we are sensitive to the needs of the children to whom we read or tell stories. Hearing them afresh, from the perspective of a parent, we may find ourselves reflecting on what the meaning behind these stories may have been. Who might have written them, and why? How is it that these particular tales are the ones to have survived the test of time?

Just as we, as we develop and mature, begin to question the attitudes and behaviours of those who have influenced our earliest years, so, too, can we reflect on the significance of those stories with which we have become familiar. We can think about what lies behind the words, the context within which the stories were told, and subsequently written down, and what the purpose of the story-teller, or writer, may have been.

It is, of course, also important for us, as Christians, that we ask such questions about the stories contained within the pages of the Bible. If we are to grow in understanding, and to help one another on the journey towards well-being, it is necessary to consider the context of each Bible story, and to look beyond the actual words to discover the meaning a story has for us today.

Stories and culture

It is often not the story itself that creates a problem, but, rather, the way in which that particular story and our particular understanding of it – as influenced by our own particular situation and life experience – come together to produce our own particular response. Many of us may have recited the poem about the magpie – the one that caused so much distress to Andy in the story above – without giving any it much thought. It is when a story we hear resonates in some way with our own experience that it takes on particular significance for us: it is then that an emotional response to the story is felt. Depending on both the content of the story and the way it relates to our own situation, the hearing of the story can be helpful and reassuring, or it can bring worry or distress.

Our cultural background also affects the way we hear and are able to respond to stories. If, when listening to Andy's distress, I had no idea what a magpie is, or had never heard the story that had upset him, then the way I chose to help him would have been very different.

When working in India with my husband a few years ago, we caught sight of a newspaper heading: 'Pangolin enters Bangalore'. Never having seen or heard the word 'pangolin' before, we had no idea whether to be pleased or worried by this news. The story lacked any meaning for us. Later that day, having asked colleagues in the hospital where we were based, we learned that we had cause neither to celebrate nor worry. For a pangolin, we discovered, is a smallish mammal, similar to an armadillo. Given the horrendous traffic conditions of Bangalore, however, we feared for the life of the vulnerable animal that had strayed within the city boundary.

Where the culture in which the story is set, or the culture of the story-teller, differs from the culture of the person who hears the story, then confusion can occur. It is especially important to bear this in mind, as we share the stories found in the pages of the Bible.

Bible stories

Bible stories are particularly open to misunderstanding or misinterpretation. That this is so should not surprise us. The most recent stories contained in the Bible were written down two thousand years ago, and much of the Hebrew Bible – our Old Testament – a long time before that. Scriptures from other traditions of faith are also ancient writings, and, as such, open to misinterpretation. All ancient scripture requires study and reflection.

Some misunderstandings are caused by the language used. A colleague told me of a book in which he had read of a child's attempt at making sense of the line of the Lord's Prayer – 'lead us not into temptation'. Not, presumably, being familiar with the word 'temptation', the child interpreted what he had heard as being, 'lead us not into Thames Station'. This is an example of trying to make sense of what is incomprehensible, although all it does, in fact, is raise further questions in the mind of the child. Why should I avoid Thames Station? Is it somewhere frightening and dangerous? Or somewhere fun and exciting; a place that this dull and boring God I have to sit still and hear about, while my friends are out playing football, does not want me to enjoy?

Confusions created by a misunderstanding of language used can have long-term effects, and many of these can be negative. Before I had learned to read for myself, I was taught at Sunday School to sing the following hymn:

When mothers of Salem
Their children brought to Jesus,
The stern disciples drove them back
And bade them depart;
But Jesus saw them ere they fled,
And sweetly smiled and kindly said,
'Suffer little children
To come unto me.'[34]

---

34 *The Psalms and Church Hymnary: revised edition*, London: Oxford University Press, [no date.] Hymn number 659. Words by William Medlen Hutchings.

Mistaking 'disciple' for 'discipline' and 'bade' for 'bad' led me, for years, to believe that followers of Jesus were nasty people. Misguided by the use of words, I heard this hymn telling me that Jesus wanted children to suffer. And, rather than being convinced by his 'sweet smile' that I might be wrong, these words, linked in my mind to my own experiences of the time, convinced me that it was safer to assume that suffering was intended than to trust a smile.

It is not, however, only the language used that can cause confusion. Bible stories are open to misinterpretation; taking them literally, rather than searching for the meaning *behind* the story, or reflecting on the reason why the story was written, can lead to painful or unhelpful conclusions. When, for example we hear the stories of people Jesus is recorded as healing, and believe that *only these people* were healed, then we are faced with huge questions about where God is in our world today, or why God chooses some for healing, and others not. We need to ask questions about why these particular stories were written down, and what those early writers were wishing to tell us about the nature and purpose of Jesus.

Many of the stories in the Bible, when taken at face value, can lead to an understanding of God that is unhelpful, or even dangerous.

As we read the stories contained within the writings of scripture – the story of God's relationship with us – we ask ourselves about the context in which the story was told. Who was telling the story? Who recorded it, and who wrote it down? What was the context in which it was written? What might have been the meaning of the story to those who chose to write it down? And what was the significance to those who, centuries later, chose to bind it within the pages of what we know today as the Bible? All this needs to be considered as we ask ourselves what such stories are saying to us in the context of our own day to day lives.

The *meaning behind the words* is what is so important. Whether listening, in a pastoral situation, to the story of a person or a group in need, or listening to the story of God as recorded in the words of scripture, we need to listen both *to* and *beyond* the words we hear.

Bible stories and pastoral care

Focusing too much on stories from the Bible can be a particular temptation for the Christian carer. Let us imagine a young woman who we have been supporting through a difficult time. She shows an interest in our faith and asks some questions about the Bible. Pleased that she seems interested in hearing the story of Jesus, we find ourselves side-tracked from *her* story, thereby missing the opportunity to help her through the problems she is dealing with.

Too much emphasis on the Bible and on faith can be unhelpful to our pastoral care. Too little emphasis, however, can be equally unhelpful.

The young woman we imagined above may be asking questions about the Bible because what she has read in its pages is contributing to her distress. She may be angry, for example, that the Jesus who healed the woman who had been bleeding for twelve years has not heard her pleas for healing. Or, maybe, remembering her violent and abusive father, she may be afraid to pray at all, because of the opening words – 'Our Father' – of the Lord's Prayer. To ignore her questions is to fail to see the connection between her story and the Bible stories she wants to discuss. And by persuading her to focus on getting better for now, and telling her that 'we can think about this again when you are well' – however well-intentioned – is to treat her as somehow less than human because of her illness or distress, and to deny the relationship of her faith to her well-being.

Andy's problem with the story of the magpie highlights another issue to consider when we use Bible stories to help in our pastoral care. Stories, as we have said above, mean different things to different people. Bible stories, with such a long history, have been interpreted and re-interpreted in so many ways, publicly in sermons and lectures and in books as well as by individuals and families who read and reflect on them.

Stories heard at church, in Bible Study group, Sunday School, or Junior Church group, are listened to within the culture of a region or nation. In addition, they are explained within the context of the theology of a particular denomination and the specific perspective of an individual congregation, and are shaped by the unique understanding of the story-teller himself or herself. Not only all that, but these stories are heard by individuals at particular moments in *their* own unique history and life experience.

A Bible story that brings meaning and purpose to one individual may raise enormous questions in the mind of another. Listening to the Parable of the Lost Sheep (St. Luke 15.4-7), for example, may lead a woman living in a remote farmhouse to a real awareness of God's concern – not just in the history of humanity – but for her in her own particular moment of need. The same story, however, may lead a rich city businessman to feel just the opposite. He may hear it as saying that God, in the days before big city business, was with his people. But, since sheep are so outwith his experience, this man comes to a very different conclusion – that God is out of touch with modern society, and thus can have no interest in him or his struggles.

This does not mean that we avoid using the Bible in our care for others. But it *does* mean that we have to use it sensitively and appropriately. Words used to bring comfort or reassurance in one situation can, if taken literally, cause upset in another. An example from my own experience makes this clear. When I first began working as a Mental Health Chaplain, I found the following words from the book of the prophet Isaiah particularly meaningful, and sometimes quoted them to a patient in distress:

> The Lord who created you says, 'Do not be afraid – I will save you. I have called you by name – you are mine (Isaiah 43.1)

Words of hope follow, echoing the story of Jesus as he stilled the storm on the lake, and reminding us that nothing can separate us form the love of God:

> When you pass through deep waters, I will be with you;
> your troubles will not overwhelm you.
>
> When you pass through fire, you will not be burnt;
> the hard trials that come will not hurt you (Isaiah 43.2)

Words of hope when experiencing the emotional problems associated with mental illness. If God can calm the storms without – as he calmed the storm to ensure the safety of his disciples out on the lake as the winds blew and the waves tossed them about – then surely he can still the storms within, our confusing emotions and our inner turmoil. Things that can seem, from time to time, too much for us to bear, *can* be coped with. The waters and the flames are not to be understood literally, but as descriptions of the feelings that can threaten to overwhelm us all.

Then, in quick succession, I was involved in the care of two individuals who were finding life especially difficult. Both ended their own lives, one by walking into the sea and drowning, the other by setting himself alight with petrol, and dying in agony among the flames. Suddenly I was angry: these words mean nothing! How can anybody read them, and find comfort?

I had to remind myself of the danger of taking words literally. If we do, they risk losing their value. Their significance to our own lives is lost.

I found comfort in the words of a hymn:

And when human hearts are breaking
under sorrow's iron rod,
then they find that selfsame aching
deep within the heart of God.[35]

However much God cares, and however much we may do our best to care for those in deep distress, we *cannot* stop the fire from burning and we *cannot* prevent the sea from drowning. That is reality. But God cares, and suffers with us. The meaning of the words on the page continues to be relevant: God *is* always with us.

This story from my experience highlights two specific difficulties that must be recognised when we use stories from the Bible in our pastoral care.

First, we must be aware of the potential problems that may arise, where the words of the story are understood as being *literally* true. If we convince ourselves that our faith must be inadequate, because we are unable to walk on water, we may fail to notice the times when God does indeed support and sustain us. Rather

---

35 *Hymns and Psalms: a Methodist and ecumenical hymnbook*, London: Methodist Publishing House, 1983. Hymn number 36. Words by Timothy Rees.

than taking stories at 'face value', we need to help each other to look beyond the words on the page to discover their meaning and significance.

And second, we need always to keep in mind the 'bigger picture'. Meaning cannot be summed up in a single story. Stories understood within the wider context of the Bible as a whole can, however, help us to discover more about our human relationship with God. Reflecting on the story of Peter's attempt to walk across the water to Jesus, within the context of God's love for each one of us, can help us, not to walk on water, but to trust in God's promise to help us as we face life's 'storms and waves'.

Searching for the messages contained within the stories of the Bible, and within all the stories we share, is an important aspect of pastoral care. As we look beyond the words of these stories, we discover meanings that offer encouragement and hope. And such hope is essential to our well-being.

Chapter Eight
What's a Yoke, Then?

Story

An Indian friend is telling me about his experience as a theological student. Thomas is in his final year of study at a college in the south Indian city of Madurai where he is training to be a pastor. At this college, much importance is given to practical work; learning by experience is a priority. While some of the students have grown up in a small farming or fishing community, the majority come from an urban background. Encouraging church workers to serve in rural areas is a priority for the college, so it provides opportunities for all students to develop at least some understanding of what daily life is like in rural India, where the vast majority of the population lives. All students, therefore, as part of their training, have to spend several weeks experiencing village life.

The college has links with several villages into which, each year, small groups of three or four students are sent to live for a college term. Villagers are asked to welcome them, and to teach them about village life. During their time in the village, the students are expected to live on the same amount of money as the basic daily wage of the villagers. They learn how to cook in the open air, a skill unfamiliar to many of them. The students are required to do any work that the villagers ask them to do, and they are encouraged to share in all aspects of village life.

During his weeks in a remote rural community, Thomas tells me, he spent a lot of his time out in the fields learning how to plough the soil and plant the rice crop. At first light, he set off each morning with a group of men and their bullock, to work for the local landowner. The back-breaking work was exhausting, he says, but working long hours is essential if the villagers are to earn enough to feed themselves and their families.

Back in college, the students were encouraged to reflect on their experience. How had they coped? What had they enjoyed?

Which aspects of daily village life had they found most challenging? What is life really like in rural India? What has Christianity to offer to poor farmers and daily labourers? What is the Good News for these people?

It is these last two questions that Thomas is keen to discuss with me. Soon he must decide where he would like to be sent by the church to work. If he were to choose to serve as a pastor in a remote, rural area, what would he do? What would be his priorities? How could he make the stories of the Bible meaningful in the lives of the people?

Living at the college in Madurai city, Thomas is aware that the parts of the Bible that help make the story of Jesus relevant to the lives of city dwellers may be hard for poor villagers to identify with. The towers of its vast, ancient temple dominate the centre of Madurai, and the city streets are always crowded with pilgrims and tourists. It is likely, therefore, that the story of Jesus getting angry with the people selling goods in the forecourts of the temple at Jerusalem will be meaningful to the people of Madurai.

Stories with a more rural flavour, however, will probably have more immediate interest to folk living in isolated villages. People aware of the need for attentive shepherding will appreciate the care of Jesus the Good Shepherd. Those who regularly face the hardships of life without access to fresh water will be keen to hear more about the man who describes himself as 'living water'. 'He came to help people like us', is what we hope they might feel.

Thomas suddenly sits upright. 'I've had an idea,' he says, beginning to sound excited. 'Remember I told you about the villagers trying to teach us to plough with that bullock they got a loan to buy?' 'Yes,' I reply. 'I'm so glad that they were able to club together to apply for that money. Just imagine how difficult all that work would be if it all had to be done by hand! And how long it would take!' 'Well,' Thomas continues, 'they told us one evening how they had trained the young bullock to pull the plough. So they'd understand exactly what Jesus means when he talks about his yoke being easy.' 'Go on,' I encourage him. And this is what he tells me.

'They got the loan to buy a young bullock to train. So it was brought to them, along with an experienced one to help it learn its work. The agreement was that the villagers hand the mature bullock back once the young one is ready for the plough. This was all new to me, but the villagers told me how hard a bullock can be to train. The best way is to have another bullock, already experienced at pulling the plough.

'They start off', Thomas continues, 'by just letting the young one tag along beside the older one. That helps it get the idea about walking up and down in a straight line. And begins to teach it about turning tight corners. Then they put a rope around its shoulders, so it gets used to being tugged and pulled a bit as it plods up and down. And only once that is going okay does the bullock get fitted with its yoke. When it first feels the weight, of course, it doesn't like it at all. So they make sure that it is the older bullock that is actually taking most of the strain – the yoke is kind of unbalanced so that the young one gets used to the weight of the yoke itself before it has to pull the plough as well. And, of course, having the experienced animal alongside helps to keep him calm: it just keeps plodding back and forth and doesn't bother about the weight, and it's not bothered by any sudden noises from the village. So gradually the young one gets the message. It learns what to do and how to respond to the commands it gets. It stops getting stressed or pulling against the yoke.'

'Do you see', says Thomas, 'how the villagers would understand about Jesus and his yoke being easy? Can you imagine the scene? Jesus walking with them in their daily life, just a step or so ahead, pulling that bit harder, so that all their problems feel just that little bit easier to bear. What a wonderful image!'

Reflection

What a wonderful image indeed! Hearing a story about a yoke makes sense to a man used to walking behind an animal pulling a plough.

How meaningful is it, though, to the farmer who drives a powerful tractor and uses a mechanical harvester? Farmers here in our country might feel that, by talking about a yoke, Jesus is just a figure from the past, irrelevant to life today. And what about those unfamiliar with the rural lifestyle? If this story is difficult for the citizens of Madurai to make sense of, in a country where animals are still yoked to a plough, how can we expect it to be meaningful to the people of Motherwell or Markinch? In countries the world over, young urban dwellers need help to understand the image, before ever they can begin to appreciate its message.

If the 'story of God', as told in the pages of the Bible, is to have significance in today's world, then we need to find ways of telling, and re-telling them, that are meaningful and significant.

Life and Work, the magazine of the Church of Scotland, in the summer of 2009, organised a competition entitled '*Parables for Today*', in conjunction with the Scottish Bible Society and the Scottish Storytelling Centre. Competition entrants were encouraged to take one of the parables told by Jesus, reflect on its meaning to them, and write a story based on present-day experience, in order to bring alive the meaning of the original parable. The aim of the competition was to encourage new ways of expressing the messages contained within the parables Jesus told.

Acting out familiar Bible stories within the context of worship is another method often used by congregations. In my own younger days, taking part in Sunday School plays, the Parable of the Good Samaritan was variously re-told with such titles as The Good Football Hooligan, The Good Punk Rocker and The Good Goth.

We have to be careful, though. Such 'updates' are not always helpful. Once a story we tell is written down and published, we can have no idea where it might be read or by whom. The inclusion of present-day details, while making a Bible story meaningful to the writer, may hide, instead of highlight, the message intended in the original. A football supporter or Goth might, with good reason, be unhappy with the implied surprise shown by the church that he, or she, is capable of showing compassion.

The purpose of telling Bible stories is to speak of God's relationship with the world he has created. Whether we read straight from the Bible, or re-tell stories in our own words, our aim is to share the good news that God cares for *all* people, and that God is here with us to help *each one of us* on the journey of life.

Telling by caring

The best way of telling people that they are loveable, and loved by God, is to love them. The best way of telling people about God's guidance and care is to support and care for each other.

The Bible teaches us that the way we relate to our neighbour is an indication of how much, or how little, we love God. John, in his first letter tells us, indeed, that we *cannot* love God if we do not love our neighbour. His words are a challenge to all who try to live Christ's way of love. Worship and praise mean nothing, the Bible teaches us, if we do not love our neighbours and seek their well-being as well as our own.

John's words also act as a reminder as to just how difficult it is for anyone to feel that God – who they have not seen – can love them, if all around them are people who reject them, avoid them or even seem not to notice them. How can anyone believe in *God's* love, without first experiencing love within *human relationship?*

On the visit to India during which I met Thomas, I also spent some time in Bangalore, the capital city of the state of Karnataka. Bangalore is a vast, and rapidly growing South Indian city, whose population size well exceeds that of the whole of Scotland. My main reason for going there was to visit a centre there, where people experiencing long-term mental illness are cared for. While in the city, though, I also had the opportunity to spend some time at a large theological college, to which men and women from all over India come, to train as pastors, counsellors and youth workers.

At evening worship on the Sunday I was there, there was a guest preacher whose sermon focussed on the purpose of the church. 'You are training to be pastors and missionaries', he told the students, 'and mission is about sharing God's love. It's a huge task. We know how small the church is in our country. We know that only about two in every hundred Indians are Christian. But God is with us and will teach us how to share his love. So never forget to pray. Always listen out for God's word. Always seek to do God's will. And remember this: God does not ask us to convert 98% of our population to believe as we do. God calls us, rather, to make real his love in the lives of *all 100%*'.[36]

As we think about our own situation here, this is an important message for us too. We do not try to persuade others to accept what we believe. Our aim, rather, is to share God's love: to enable each and every person in the community around us to experience the love of God in their own life.

36 Words spoken during sermon preached at United Theological College, Bangalore, South India, on Palm Sunday, 2008.

Caring pastorally

The purpose of pastoral care, as defined in the chapter *Swimming Pigeons,* is to encourage and enable the well-being of individuals and of communities.

Earlier, we thought about how the church can work with other organisations to improve mental health and well-being. By working together in partnership, we can make use of the particular contribution brought by each partner, and thus improve the care that can be offered. It is, therefore, important that we recognise the specific contribution of the pastoral care of the church.

It is the reason *why* we care that makes pastoral care distinctive. It is our belief that God is with us, and that – through our caring – God's love and justice can be enjoyed by all people, that is at the heart of all we do. This is why, throughout this book, the need to *reflect* on our faith is stressed.

We do not, of course, care *only* because God asks us to. Our motivation to care is not so that we can earn God's favour or reward. We care because our hope is that, through loving human relationships, all people will be led towards the fullness of life that only *God's* love can bring.

The motivation of faith offers two distinctive dimensions to care that is *pastoral.*

First, our understanding that all life is lived in relationship with God, who is both Creator and Redeemer of the world, challenges us to think beyond the immediate situation to the bigger picture of what it means to live in God's world.

In a moment of crisis, of course, or when disaster strikes, an urgent response is what is needed. When lives are in danger, there is no time to ponder the meaning of events: we just get on with meeting the needs of the moment. As we live day by day, however, we make time to reflect on what the Bible teaches us, and to discuss with one another what should be the priorities in our lives. Our faith in the God of love and justice is our guide, as we consider how best to love our neighbour and to 'let justice flow like a stream' through our local area. As we ask, in prayer, in Bible Study, and in discussion together, 'how might God see this situation?', we discover appropriate ways of sharing God's gifts in the community around us.

Related to this is the second aspect of caring that is *pastoral*: our awareness that God is with us. God is with us in all that we do, in all our relationships; with us and supporting us. Whether or not we *talk* of God, our faith tells us that – as we think and plan, and as we listen and support – God *is* with us.

These pastoral perspectives have an important contribution to make to any planning and action to improve well-being. Insights arising from faith need to be heard alongside ideas rooted in the understandings of social welfare, justice and mental health improvement.

Caring by telling

Talking about our faith, then, is an important aspect of our pastoral care. In discussion, and planning, to develop a new service within a local community, for example, the Christian perspective on what people need in order to live well needs to be heard. When, as a church, we meet with other local groups to decide how to respond to a particular problem in our neighbourhood, what the Bible tells us about justice and compassion can give a helpful perspective. It is important, whether others present in such plan-making share our faith or not, that we use the gift of faith that God has given us to shed light on the issues being considered.

We also use the gift of our faith as we offer care and support in times of need. Sometimes, we will speak of our faith: often, though, this will not be appropriate. But our faith is always there, as our guide and support, enabling us to give the love, or the compassion, that is required. Our faith is with us, reminding us that God loves those we are trying to help, and that God understands their need. Trusting that God is present with us in each caring relationship enables us to help one another on the journey to well-being.

So, therefore, we should not be shy of talking about God.

The focus of this chapter, with its story about a story from the Bible, is on *talking about God* as one of the dimensions of our pastoral care.

Loving our neighbour will sometimes require us to speak about God, and about the help that God gives on the journey of life. In doing so, however, it is important not to impose our own understandings and beliefs, or to persuade others to think as we do. We follow the example of Jesus, who spoke words of encouragement and of challenge to the crowds who gathered to listen to him. His teaching ministry stirred in his hearers the desire to discover for themselves the new life that he promised is God's gift for all people. Our hope is that, by hearing us talk of God's care and concern, others may choose to ask for God's help, and experience for themselves how relationship with God can bring new purpose and hope in their lives.

Telling that God is with us – with each individual

St. Matthew records Jesus as inviting all who are tired and weary to come to him and find rest (St. Matthew 11.8-30). Such rest is not, however, a lazy abandonment of responsibilities. There is work to be done by the followers of Jesus. In Jesus' words here, there *is* a load to carry and there *is* a yoke to be worn. The rest that Jesus offers is not freedom from our responsibilities, but *his help with them*: 'For the yoke I will give you is easy, and the load I will put on you is light'.

As Thomas, in the story at the beginning of this chapter, realised, this image of the yoke, with Jesus taking the heavier strain, can help us to see the relationship between our faith and our everyday life. Trusting in Jesus, and following him faithfully, seen from the point of view of this image of the 'easy yoke', leads us to active involvement in the life of our community. The farmer with faith must still plough the fields; faith is no 'magic solution' or escape from the world. The farmer and his family are dependent on the crops that are grown for their survival. The sense of responsibility to provide for family and community *increases*, rather than decreases, when an individual finds relationship with Jesus and tries to follow in his way.

Understanding the image of the 'easy yoke' in this way, however, may be difficult for those who may be thinking about faith, or hearing about Jesus, for the first time. How often, over coffee after a church service, do we hear comments that a sermon was 'good' because it was entertaining, or full of stories? And how many of us, if indeed we think at all about what a preacher or minister has said on a Sunday morning, find that we have remembered the story that was told, but have forgotten what it was that the story was told to clarify or explain? If this is true for those of us who already have faith, how much more will it be the case for those for whom all thoughts about God and belief are new?

Telling this story, then, may – as mentioned earlier in this reflection – be unhelpful, or discourage the hearer from finding out more about faith. It may be understood as an old story – which it certainly is – but also as an out of date story and, as such, irrelevant in the life of the hearer – which it most certainly is not. If a story gets in the way of its message, then, it may be better not to tell it.

This is one of the main reasons why knowing the *context* of each Bible story is so important. If we do not take the time to find out why a story was told so long ago, and who were the people who heard it, then it may be almost impossible for us to identify the message it was trying to convey.

Think, for example, about the story of the Israelites crossing the Red Sea in safety. It is a part of the epic story of how the people of Israel were freed from slavery in Egypt and led through the wilderness to freedom in the Promised Land. Understood as a story teaching us about our relationship with God, the message is as true for us today as it was for the first people who heard it: God loves and cares for all who believe in him, and leads us towards fullness of life.

Told in isolation, however, the story of the crossing of the Red Sea may be heard a bit like those stories of Cowboys and Indians that some of us may recall from our childhood: the good guys win and the bad guys lose. On one occasion when I was leading worship, and the story of the escape from Egypt and the crossing of the Red Sea was the Bible passage being read, I was challenged angrily by a young man who was hearing this story for the first time. 'I thought you said God loves *everybody*', he said. 'But that story proves God is just callous and violent, and that he's only concerned about the people who say they believe in him. If that's what God is really like, I don't want anything to do with him.'

He was right to be angry. If God were to help only his own 'special people', and be happy to wipe out anybody who treats them badly, then he is not the God of love and justice in whom we put our trust.

When we talk of God, our words must – at the very least – not turn people away from relationship with him. What we say about God can encourage people to want to experience his love in their own lives.

The 'yoke' we bear as Christians, therefore, includes the responsibility to lead others to relationship with God. And we thank God that the yoke is 'easy', because we walk alongside Jesus and he helps us with all we do and say.

The yoke that brought freedom then

Why, though, did Jesus use this particular image, when he spoke to the crowd who gathered to listen to his words? What was he trying to tell them about their relationship with God? Being aware of what Jesus meant, when he talked to *those people then* about his yoke being easy, can enable us to make the *message* of the story clear, even to those whose first response is to ask us, 'what's a yoke, then?'

The yoke – the burden borne by the crowds who came to listen to Jesus – was the burden of the Law. The Jews who lived and worked in the villages Jesus visited were bound by the legalism created by the Scribes and the Pharisees who, over the centuries, had turned the Ten Commandments into innumerable laws. The people were taught that obeying these endless laws was essential to their faith. If the sacrifice they took to the temple was not perfect – a pigeon with a damaged wing, for example – they would be refused access or forced into buying another. Worshipping God was 'out of bounds' to those who could not comply with the legalism of the time.

But Jesus wanted them to see that they can all have 'free access' to God. Relationship with God cannot be earned by anyone; it is freely given out of God's generous love. God desires the worship of a thankful heart, and asks them to show kindness and mercy to one another. These, and not animal sacrifice or obedience to the Law, are what will enable them to live in relationship with God.

'I am here to help you', was what Jesus was telling the crowds who gathered to hear him speak. 'Take *my* yoke. Follow me, and learn how to love one another. Do this and you will find God'. The obedience that Jesus asked of them was not legalistic: it was about taking responsibility for each other's well-being. 'Love your neighbour' was what Jesus expected of them.

The yoke that brings freedom today

We may not be first century Jews weighed down by legalism. But, in today's world, there are many people who believe that God's love has to be earned. Some people have been taught that they must somehow prove themselves to be worthy of God's love, before they can come to worship him in church or receive his blessing through the sharing of bread and wine.

There are people in today's society who need to find freedom, not from slavery in Egypt, but from enslavement to the desire for wealth or for power and status. Many require help to escape from the pain of hunger or homelessness. Most of us need encouragement and support to break the bonds we have to guilt or past regrets.

Hearing that God is with us *within* our daily lives and working alongside us, to share in our burdens and our cares, can bring reassurance and renew hope. Discovering that God is leading us, and ready to teach us and encourage us on our journey through life, can bring new purpose, as we ask ourselves about the meaning of our life or what life on earth is all about.

Asking 'what's a yoke, then?' can be the start of a journey towards faith. The words of Jesus, told with awareness of the original context, and explained in a way relevant to the present situation of the listener, can lead to exciting new discoveries about life lived in relationship with God.

All of us, for a whole range of different reasons, can experience the feeling of being separated from God's love. This story of the yoke that Jesus tells us he shares with us helps to remind us of his commitment to being alongside of us. Jesus has chosen to accompany us, to support us on the journey through life and to guide us on the path to fullness of life.

This can bring hope to each of us, as individuals. God cares enough to guide each one of us through the unique problems and challenges that we face. This is good news that is, indeed, worth telling.

That God is with us, here and now, in the midst of life, is good news for each individual. It is also good news for humanity as a whole. The 'field' that we 'plough', yoked as we are to the God who supports us and encourages us, is the place where we live and work. The yoke that binds us to our Saviour binds us also to those around us in this community. Bound together by God's love, we are enabled to care for each other and encouraged to discover – together – the way that leads to well-being.

Telling that God is with us – in loving community

Hearing that our relationship with God is like that of an 'easy yoke', by which God has chosen to bind himself to us in shared commitment, can be a life-enhancing experience. It does not, however, only bring encouragement and hope to the individual listener. Relationship with the God of love challenges each one who discovers it to seek such encouragement and hope for others also.

Our relationship with God and our concern for the well-being of others are closely inter-twined. This is what makes our care *pastoral*. It is our faith in the God of love that motivates us to love our neighbour, and it is through loving our neighbour that our relationship with God can deepen, and, thus, our own life be enriched. Our own well-being is closely linked to that of the people around us, just as theirs is bound up with ours.

This inter-relationship between individual and community well-being is highlighted in many of the Gospel stories that tell of people healed by Jesus. An example of such a story is the one in which we read about a man, described as suffering from a 'dreaded skin-disease', usually understood as referring to leprosy (St. Mark 1.40-45). The man, we hear, approaches Jesus, and asks to be made clean. Jesus reaches out and touches him, and the man is freed from the disease. But that is not the end of the story: Jesus tells him to go to the priest and to ask to be examined by him. It seems that it is the priest, and not Jesus, nor the man himself, who can declare that he is now healed.

So what is going on here? The man would have been in considerable pain. We can appreciate how much he would long to be rid of this suffering. Leprosy results in a numbing of feeling, thus making people affected by the disease susceptible to injury. For a woman cooking over an open fire, getting burnt is a real danger. Nerves in fingers affected by the disease do not sense the intensity of the heat; there is no 'ouch! factor' to make her pull her hands away. Walking barefoot on rough and stony ground, numbed feet do not notice cuts and bruises, and before long wounds are caused, leading to infection.

Leprosy, however, does not only result in physical pain. Emotional pain may be a greater cause of distress, because people living with leprosy are often shunned by others in their local community. Even today, with new awareness of the causes of leprosy, and of the ways of controlling its symptoms, those who live with the condition are often feared and rejected.

Jesus, we are told, stretched out his hand and touched the man with leprosy. We can imagine everyone there at the scene recoiling in horror. By touching the man, Jesus was making himself ritually unclean, and thereby – according to the belief of the time – cutting himself off from God. It seems, though, that this was of no concern to Jesus. Indeed, we would expect this to be so, given his challenge to the legalism of the time, and his contempt for the rituals identified as being 'essential' before people could attend worship in synagogue or temple.

As we reflect on this story, we see that it is not only the pain of his symptoms that makes the man turn to Jesus for help. When he asked Jesus to make him clean, he would have known only too well that his disease was considered to be the result of sin. People who were sick were forbidden to enter places of worship; illness was believed to be a result of sin. Thus, until the priest could be sure that the man was free from disease, he would deny him access to worship. Until the man had been allowed by the priest to offer a sacrifice, his relationship with God – according to the understanding of the time – could not be restored. And without such restored relationship with God, he would remain cut off from his family, and from the support of the wider community.

Jesus, by the way he lived and taught, made it clear that he rejected the idea that illness is punishment for sin; that the one who is sick is to blame for their illness. He also, as we know, challenged the belief that God does not welcome and love those who have made mistakes or done wrong in their lives. His teaching makes it clear that God's love is for *everyone*, and his forgiveness freely available to us all. In sending the man he has freed from leprosy to the priest, however, he is recognising that, within the cultural understanding of the time, this ritual must take place, before the man can be welcomed again into his family and his community

Released from the symptoms of his disease, the man found freedom from his pain. Just as important for his well-being, though, was the re-establishment of relationship. The man was now free to return to life within his community, and able to enter into the presence of God once more. Responding, then, in the way he did, Jesus encouraged this man, whose life had been marred by leprosy, to discover again what is means to live *well*.

It was not only the man himself, however, who was helped to find well-being. Broken relationships also need healing. The people must welcome the man once more into their midst, before they, too, can experience the well-being he has found.

This story helps us to understand the inter-relationship between individual, and community, well-being. It is, therefore, significant to life in our local communities today.

To tell or not to tell?

This story of this man who had suffered with leprosy being restored to life in his community has a lot to say to us about how we can enable each other to experience well-being when going through a period of mental illness.

Living with leprosy severed the man's relationship with the people in his community and denied him access to his place of worship. Mental illness, too, can make us feel cut off from God.

The man with leprosy was shunned by the people around him. Those of us who have experienced mental illness speak of feeling misunderstood, or ignored, sometimes even by the people we thought were closest to us.

We need to think carefully, however, about *when* and *how* to tell this story and others like it. Told in isolation – separate from the wider context of the whole life and teaching of Jesus – stories of 'healings' can confuse, puzzle, or upset those who hear them. Told in isolation – separate from the wider context of pastoral care – hearing such stories can lead people to despair rather than hope, as they turn away from the Jesus who seems to have no care or compassion for them in *their* time of illness or need.

It is important, therefore, that we always take time to reflect on the *appropriateness* of telling stories from the Bible, or stories about faith.

If, by telling a story from the Bible now – in this particular place, at this particular time – we can help *this particular individual* on his or her journey towards well-being, then it is a story worth sharing. At the wrong time, or in the wrong place, however, and – especially – if we are not able to provide any necessary care or practical support, then it is better that the story is left untold – at least for now.

Healing from symptoms

The *message* of the story about the man who had leprosy is that relationship with Jesus brings new life and hope.

If we focus only on the relief from symptoms in the story, we risk encouraging people to expect 'magic solutions' from God. Then, when prayer, or attendance at a service of healing, does not bring them freedom from *their* symptoms, they may begin to doubt that God loves them.

There *are* occasions when people are released from disease, or illness, through prayer or the laying on of hands. When such apparently miraculous healing does take place, however, there will be many who will ask, 'Why him – or her – and not me?' No doubt those who heard news of the man freed from his leprosy asked the same question. 'Unexplainable cures' may be a cause of celebration for some. Sensitivity is required, though, if others are not to feel that that their faith is not strong enough, that they are not worthy to receive God's help, or that God is ignoring their need. 'She – or he – must be more important to God', or 'God does not love *me*' are thoughts likely to go through the minds of the many people who never experience such release from the symptoms of their illness. If one person's 'healing' adds to the pain of others, then it cannot lead to well-being. No wonder Jesus told the man freed from his leprosy to keep quiet!

The issue of 'miraculous healing' is not the topic of this book. Such experience is acknowledged as a part of the Gospel story of Jesus, and as one aspect within the tradition of the church. Our focus, however, is on the *whole* story of Jesus as Emmanuel: Jesus as *God with us*, bearing the yoke with us as we travel life's journey.

The pro-active and re-active pastoral care that is reflected upon within this book is motivated and sustained by our belief that *God is with us*. God's promise is made clear to us in the story of Jesus and the yoke he shares with us. God is with us to enable and encourage us in times of difficulty. God is with us, *in and through life*, as help and as guide.

This does not mean that relieving symptoms is not our concern. Prevention of illness and disease is a significant part of pro-active pastoral care. We can do much to ensure that our environment is free from pollution, and that homes and factories, schools and churches are safe to be in and accessible by all. As Christians, we are active in many different aspects of health care. Encouraging people to seek appropriate medical care is as important as supporting them by our prayers.

Also essential to our pastoral care, however, is what we do to ensure – when pain and suffering does come – that nobody is denied the help and support that they need, and that everyone is enabled to live well, even within the experience of illness. As we seek to provide what is needed, we trust that God will guide us. However inadequate our caring may sometimes seem, God can use it to free those who suffer into new life and new hope.

Mental illness and God's love

By looking *beyond* this one particular story in the life of Jesus, and reflecting on its message, within the context of other aspects of his teaching, we can encourage one another to talk to God in prayer, and to ask God *themselves* for the help they need. We can reassure each other that there is nothing we need to *do*; we do not need to 'earn the right' to talk with God. All we need do is ask.

The requirement of ritual cleansing was for *then*; other stories from the life of Jesus make it clear that all who turn to God for help will receive it. In his teaching about the Holy Spirit, Jesus makes it clear that relationship with God is not merely to be found within synagogue or temple. God's love is freely available; 'ask and you will receive'.

Asking for God's help means also seeking help within the community around us. God has given us each other. But turning to others for help can be difficult for us when we are going through a time of mental illness. People going through a period of depression may feel unable to ask for help they need. Many people who become anxious will be reluctant to admit their need of support, fearing the rejection that may result when others become aware of their mental illness. Some of the most vulnerable among us may be convinced that nobody cares about them. So, as people who believe that God knows our need before we ask, *we*, in our caring relationships, can try always to be sensitive and 'in tune' with the people around us.

Mental illness raises issues for many people. The causes of some forms of mental illness remain unclear. Brought up, as we are, within the western interpretation of life – that everything has a cause that can be explained – it can be hard to accept that our particular difficulties seem to have no specific cause. Many kinds of illness *can* be explained; we ate improperly cooked meat, or got chilled after a thorough soaking in the rain. Identifying specific causes of *mental* illnesses, however, can be much more problematic.

Unable to find a cause, it becomes all too easy to believe that we, ourselves, are responsible for the way we are feeling. So, when supporting people going through a period of mental illness, it is especially important that we assure them that they themselves are not to blame for their illness.

Some people believe that God is punishing them by their illness. This may be because, sometimes, it can be easier to believe in a God who would punish us, than to accept the seemingly random chance of '*me*' developing schizophrenia, or being susceptible to extreme mood swings. Feelings of guilt about past wrong-doings can convince us that illness must be a punishment, and can, indeed, cause us to feel distant from God.

Believing that our illness is a punishment from God can, in some circumstances, be triggered by the symptoms of the illness. Depression, for example, making us feel worthless and unloveable, can lead us to believe that we *deserve* God's punishment. Sometimes, however, it is what we have been told about God that contributes to our distress. Memories of Bible stories heard in Sunday School long ago, or inappropriate teaching from the church, can lead to the conviction that illness is, indeed, God's punishment.

The God of love does not bring illness to anyone as punishment. Our faith that tells us this, but our feelings can make it hard for us to accept that 'God loves even me'. How many of us, when things go wrong in our lives, ask the question 'why?' At such times, we are rarely looking for a cause or seeking a rational explanation. 'Why me?' 'Why now?' 'Why this?' are questions we ask when life feels hard, and problems lead us to wonder about the meaning of life.

How we *feel* about life is a guide – but not always an accurate guide. Most of us know, only too well, how easy it can be, when things are going well and we are feeling positive about life, to miss the early signals that a friend is feeling ignored or a relationship is becoming tense. We are aware, too, of occasions when, at a family gathering or in a meeting with colleagues, we have blamed others present for the tension in the room, failing to notice the effect of our own over-enthusiasm or impatience.

All of us, at least from time to time, experience this 'mismatch' between our feelings and the reality of what is going on within any relationship. This is as true for relationships between communities, racial groups and nations as it is in relationships between individuals.

It is also true for our relationship with God. Feelings can be aroused in worship: at such times, we need to remind ourselves that awareness of God's presence requires us to respond with more than emotion. Celebrating God's love for us means sharing that love with others. *Feeling* close to God needs to be balanced with the responsibilities of faith. *Feeling* distant from God, or separated from his love, is also an emotion that can be challenged by faith: God, we can trust, will never separate himself from any of us.

Trusting that God is present with us, even when life is so painful or difficult that it *feels* that God has abandoned us, is an important aspect of faith. Sometimes, we can challenge our own feelings with our own faith. Often, however, it is the *faith of the people around us*, and *their* trust in God, that sustains us through the painful feelings of isolation or abandonment. Two lines in a hymn put this so well:

> I will hold the Christ-light for you
> In the night-time of your fear.[37]

37 *Church Hymnary,* Fourth edition, Norwich: Canterbury Press, 2005. Hymn number 694. Words by Richard A.M. Gillard.

In our pastoral care, as we offer practical support, or listen to people's worries and concerns, we also sustain them by *our* faith.

This is especially important when supporting anyone who is struggling with problems associated with mental illness. This is because the symptoms of illness can make it difficult to maintain relationships. People living with depression frequently talk of a 'brick wall' that comes between them and their friends or family, making communication virtually impossible. And the same is true in their relationship with God. 'The link feels broken', they may say. Or 'I want to talk to God about how I feel – but I just *can't*'.

At times like these, it is trusting that the light *is* there – because someone has promised to hold it for us in our darkness – that helps keep hope alive.

God is with us: well-being for all

God is with us. That is the message that we tell. We tell this message in words, as we share the story of God's love for all people. We tell it as we share God's love through our care and concern for neighbours near and far. We tell it, too, as we live our lives within the vision of hope that our faith tells us is for all the world.

It is our faith that gives us this vision of how life will be when God's love is experienced by all people. And it is this vision that motivates how we live. We discover what life can – and one day will – be like through the stories in the Bible.

Prophets foretold a time when the lion will lie down with the lamb, and the weapons we have developed – our modern-day spears and swords – will be transformed to be used to feed people, and to bring peace to the world. Jesus tells us of the Kingdom of God, begun here on earth at the time of his birth. God's Kingdom, Jesus says, is like a wonderful feast, at which all are welcome: no-one will go hungry when God's love is shared. God's Kingdom is like a vast tree, in and under whose branches all people will live at peace. Nobody will be shunned or excluded, ignored or rejected. All will be welcome: valued for being who they are. Everyone will feel *at home*.

The time when the Kingdom will come *in all its glory* is in God's hands, not ours: the *fullness* of life promised by God gives hope for the future.

Our vision of hope, however, is not *only* for the future. God's love is with us *now*. God's love is for sharing *now*. Well-being can be achieved in the here and now, as we challenge injustice, share resources and do all that God's call to 'love your neighbour' asks of us.

The vision God offers us, of what life in his Kingdom can be like – on earth as it is in heaven – gives meaning and purpose to life's journey. The Bible teaches us – as Christian Aid's 'strap-line', 'We believe in life before death', so clearly puts it – that we are to do all we can, in the here and now, to seek well-being for all.

God *is* with us. He promises to care for us as he leads us on the journey of life and to share our burdens as he gives us the 'easy yoke'. God's presence with us brings hope and offers new life. Together with God – and together with others in the places we live – we can transform these places into communities of hope, in which each one feels truly at home, and everybody experiences well-being.

Chapter Nine
You God Talk, Yes?

Story

It's Saturday morning and I am, as usual each weekend, in the adult ward of the psychiatric hospital. I'm sitting on a sofa in the day room, drinking coffee and talking with a group of patients. Over at the table, two men are playing 'Scrabble'. I've been in the ward for a good part of the morning; I had come early today to meet with Angela, who had phoned last night, sounding very upset. She is looking a lot more relaxed now, and is curled up in the armchair by the window, engrossed in a magazine that one of the nurses brought in for her. Other people, I know, will be in the dormitories, stretched out on their beds. A few will be in the dining area, having a late breakfast.

The 'Scrabble' players interrupt our conversation. They disagree about the spelling of the word one has just placed on the board, and ask us which of them is correct. 'Say I'm right and I'll let you all have a bit of that chocolate my brother brought in for me,' says Graham. 'Hey, don't believe him,' laughs Mohammed, 'he ate it all himself last night'.

A young woman, Shabhana, appears at the door, and looks anxiously around. I smile at her, but she turns her head away. I wonder, again, if she is depressed, or whether she might be feeling afraid about something. Last Saturday, when I was here, I had gone into the women's dormitory to ask if she would like to talk, but she had indicated that she would prefer to be alone. And I know that the staff are worried about her: she has been here for over a week now and has not spoken to anyone.

I look across at Shabhana again. She is still there, leaning against the door frame. I smile once again, and her gaze goes down to the floor. Joanne shifts along the sofa, making space for her, and pats the cushion. But still she stands silently. Mohammed looks up and calls softly to her: 'Ashun' ['please come in' in Bengali language]. But she remains where she is.

Angela puts down her magazine and stretches. 'Anyone for another cuppa?' she asks, and several people nod. She goes out to the kitchen to boil the kettle, and comes back through with coffee jar and tea bags. A few minutes later, when everyone is settled, I notice that Shabhana has moved quietly into the day room, and is watching us all intently. Joanne holds up her cup, and looks at her questioningly. Shabhana remains silent, but signs that she does not want a drink.

I turn back to Joanne and the others, and we continue our conversation. A few minutes later, I feel a hand on my shoulder. I look round, and smile again at Shabhana. This time, she does not turn away. She leans her head gently against mine, and whispers, 'You God talk, yes?'

I try not to show my surprise, and reply, in a voice as quiet as hers, 'Yes'. She smiles. And whispers another question: 'You come, yes?' 'Yes', I reply, and begin to stand up. She takes my hand, and leads me from the room. We walk silently along the corridor to the dormitory, and go in. She leads me to her bed, and says, 'You sit, yes?' I sit. She climbs onto the bed beside me, crosses her legs, and takes both my hands in hers. I wait. 'We pray, yes?' she asks. 'Yes', I reply. 'We pray now.'

She covers her head with the end of her sari, and bows low. She begins to pray, speaking in her own Bengali language. I listen to the words, recognising only that she is asking for help. I close my eyes and begin to pray silently: 'God, help Shabhana: be with her now. I have no idea what she needs. Or what she is asking for. But help her – please. And help me, too, God. Help me to understand. Tell me what to say, and what to do.'

After a while, Shabhana stops praying, but continues to hold my hands in hers. We sit in silence until I feel her gentle squeeze. I look into her eyes and smile. She smiles back. 'God help me, yes?' she asks. 'Yes', I reply. The word is echoed back to me: 'Yes!', she says with confidence. 'God help me, yes!'

She puts her arms around me, and we embrace each other. Then she climbs down from her bed, and leads me back to the day room. She walks with me to where I had been sitting on the sofa, then moves away, finding herself a chair in the corner.

The special time is over. A moment in which God was especially close. A moment in which God's love was experienced in the silence, and felt through our touch. I sense that – for both of us – trust in God has been renewed and hope rekindled.

Reflection

One brief moment, of course, could not solve Shabhana's problems. But it was, nonetheless, a significant step on her journey towards well-being.

Simply *being there* with her, and indicating my openness to Shabhana's need for affection and touch – as well as for prayer – enabled her to begin to express how she was feeling and talk about her difficulties.

Human contact is essential for health. Friendship is necessary for our well-being. Our presence – our *being there* – 'says' to the person in need or distress: 'you are not alone'. Even when we feel at a total loss about what to do or say, our *being there* can bring comfort, and renew hope in the other.

Why did Shabhana choose me? Other people had tried to communicate with her, but she had been unable to respond to their concern. Like most of the patients and all but one of the staff, I was unable to talk to her in her native Bengali language. And it was only after our short time together that Shabhana agreed to meet with the nursing auxiliary employed also to work as translator in the ward.

It was because Shabhana had discovered that I 'God talk' that she sought my help. Only much later did I find out how she had listened to conversations about me between some of the Bangladeshi patients and had learned, from hearing what they said, that my role in the ward was that of Chaplain.

Shabhana is a Muslim and I am a Christian, but her awareness of our shared recognition of need for God's help is what led her to seek me out. Prayer brought us together, despite the difference of our faith and the lack of a common language. Neither of us had any idea what the other was praying about, or for. But our shared experience of 'God talk' reminded us of our shared humanity.

Need for contact with God, and need for human contact: it was these that brought Shabhana and I together. When these needs were met – for however short a moment – she was then able to find the courage to seek out the help that she needed. That brief moment, of prayer and embrace, marked the beginning of Shabhana's long journey of recovery from illness and towards a renewed sense of well-being.

Being there: committed presence

A major aspect of this book is its emphasis on faith being our motivation and guide. It is our faith that commits us to following the example of Jesus: to living as we believe God would have us live. And it is our commitment to God's way that motivates us to care.

Trusting that God is present among us is what enables us to share his love. We need God with us to help us love our neighbour.

God shares his love through our human care for each other. The pro-active and re-active pastoral care that is the contribution of the church to community well-being is what we believe Jesus asks of us when he tells us to love God and to love our neighbour.

Loving means both caring *about* and caring *for* ourselves. Loving means both caring *about* and caring *for* other people. Some of us need caring *for* throughout our lives. *All* of us need to be cared *for* at various stages in our life, including the times when we face illness, uncertainty, or other difficulty. And *all of us*, throughout our lives, need to be *cared about*.

As humans, we thrive on good relationships. We need companions. We need friends. We feel valued when others choose to spend time with us. Knowing that other people are there with us can make many problems bearable, and bring light into even the darkest of situations.

Caring *about* one other is what we do, day by day, in our pastoral care. We support and encourage one another on the journey of life, and do all we can to ensure that the resources and facilities necessary for living well are available to, and accessible by, everyone in our community.

Caring *for* others is often necessary only for a limited period. The neighbour, newly home from hospital, will need food brought in, or help with keeping her house clean, until she feels stronger and more able to cope. The man who comes to our church asking about help for his teenage son, who has started to take illegal drugs, will be relieved to hear from us that a support group meets in our church hall. He may, however, reject any further offers to help, interpreting them as an indication that we doubt his ability as a father.

Caring *for* one another requires great sensitivity: no-one should ever feel devalued through the care they receive. The purpose of care is always to *encourage well-being*. That is why, as we have stressed throughout this book, *reflection* is so important. Caring *for* others means ensuring – as far as we can identify, through prayer, and discussion, and knowledge of the situation – that the care we offer will enable *this particular person* in *this particular situation* to resolve, or to cope with, the *particular problem* that faces them at *this particular time*.

Whether our pastoral care is caring *for* others, or caring *about* them, such care requires our committed presence. *Being there* is essential to the pro-active and re-active pastoral care that encourages and enables well-being.

Rooted in our community, we are *present*; ready and willing to do what is required, as and when help is needed. Rooted in our community, the church can work in partnership with others, to ensure that it becomes a place in which everyone is given the opportunity to live well.

Being there: shared presence

Our *being there* within our local community is a presence that is *shared*.

The pastoral care of the church can be described as 'faith in action'. Such activity, however, is never done alone. We do, of course, offer help as individuals, as well as through any resources or activities provided in or by the church. But it is because we worship together, pray together, and study the Bible together, that we are able to give encouragement and support to our colleagues and neighbours. We benefit from each other's friendship; our Christian friends can challenge our beliefs, and can offer us the insights of their faith. It is the prayerful support of our Christian companions that sustains us when caring becomes particularly difficult or challenging.

Thinking of pastoral care as 'faith in action' also helps to remind us that *God is always present*, in and through all we do and say. The decisions we make are not ours alone: God is with us to guide our thinking. The care that we share with our neighbour in need is not ours alone: God is with us to share his love. In the companionship and friendship we offer, we are not alone: God is present in all our relationships.

Being there in our community, however, extends beyond our presence as individuals and as a congregation. It also extends beyond partnership with any other congregations and church denominations within our local area. We are in partnership with all who work to develop the well-being of our community.

Without partnership, those who provide care are likely to become remote and powerful figures. We see this happening, at national level, when policies are made without consultation with those who work at the 'grass roots' or the 'coal face'. Tensions build up and relationships begin to break down. Similar problems occur where a congregation decides that 'we know best', or when the church believes that it can offer something that is 'better' than what any other agency can provide: relationships with other caring organisations can then turn sour.

The dimension of our faith gives a specific, and vitally important, aspect to the care offered within any community: it is important, therefore, that the insights of faith are shared. But many other aspects are also necessary, to ensure that everyone in our community is to experience well-being. It is as the church develops *partnerships* with other organisations and agencies that we can work – act *together* – to create communities of well-being.

Partnership: being alongside

When it is *we* who are the ones providing the care, or support, working together in partnership reminds us of our common humanity and our inter-dependence. Such partnership enables the development of health-inspiring relationships and helps, too, to prevent us from becoming proud of what we are able to offer.

When it is *we* who are the *ones in need*, partnership with those who are helping us can preserve our dignity and value as human beings. Being accepted as partners in a *caring relationship* encourages and enables our journey towards well-being.

Partnership with those requiring care, help, or support, is essential, so that we offer, not merely what is possible to provide, but is what is *required* to enable well-being.

Working together, as partners with people in distress, requires that we risk making ourselves vulnerable. In our pastoral care, we do not stand on the shore by the 'Sea of Suffering' or the 'Firth of Fear', and throw out advice, or suggestions, to people who are struggling to survive in the waters of confusion and distress. We jump in with them, and swim alongside them to help them keep afloat. But we do not do this alone. We have our life-belt. And this life-belt we wear is attached firmly to the network of guidance and support that is available to us through the partnerships we develop. Our life-belt, too, links us to the help and the guidance of God. Pastoral care is, as said above, not offered in isolation, but in partnership. And if we do not take care of ourselves, then we are of little use to others. If we rush into the water without our life-belt, we risk everyone being sucked down to the depths. 'Love your neighbour *as yourself*' is what Jesus asks of us. Relying on the community of faith, and trusting in the presence of God, we can remain secure, even in our vulnerability.

Being there through times of pain and darkness means shedding our 'status' as carer, and being *ourselves* within our 'role' as 'visiting elder' or 'deacon'. A book by John Swinton, who writes extensively about faith and mental illness, focuses on the value of simply *being there*, and being *ourselves*, as we try to help those who struggle. '*Resurrecting the person*',[38] is a book about finding new life and new hope, even while living with the symptoms of mental illness. Its sub-title – *friendship and the care of people with mental health problems* – emphasises what is essential to the re-discovery of hope: the presence of *friends*. Having someone we trust, with whom we can open up and talk about our worries, can make our pain more bearable and give our lives new meaning and purpose.

While working as a Mental Health Chaplain, it was the 'status' of employee within the NHS that permitted me to enter wards,

---

38 Swinton, John, *Resurrecting the person: friendship and the care of people with mental health problems*, Nashville: Abingdon Press, 2000.

visit day centres, and to talk with the people I met there. It was this 'status', and my identity as a member of the mental health care team, that enabled vulnerable people to agree to meet with me, or to invite me into their homes. It was the training I received in preparation for that role, and the on-going opportunities to learn, that helped me to know about the wide range of mental health problems and to understand some of the methods of treating them.

But it was neither 'status' nor 'role' that enabled me to *care*. Only when I began to shed that role and to 'be myself' did people begin to trust me, and start to tell me the stories of their lives.

It was not difficult for me to find ways of working in partnership with the people I was there to help. The hospital in which Shabhana was a patient serves an area in which there is a large population of people who have settled in the UK from Bangladesh. In the community around the hospital were also living families from the Caribbean and from West Africa. So I had the opportunity to learn from patients about their many different cultures, as well as about the problems experienced by people who leave all that is familiar behind, in order to find security and freedom in another land. I attended evening classes, held in the local primary school, trying to learn some basic skills in the Bengali language. When Mohammed – one of the 'Scrabble' players in the story at the start of this chapter – and one of the other Bangladeshi patients discovered this, they offered to practice with me on my visits to the ward. With encouragement, and a little help from me, they then produced a mini-dictionary of words relevant to life in hospital, which came to be used by both staff and patients.

Working in partnership, and developing health-enhancing relationships with the people we want to help, also makes it possible for them to keep a sense of control. When life feels chaotic, and circumstances seem to be 'all against us', it is important that we still feel that we have some control over the decisions we make. Enabling people to talk through plans, and to bounce their ideas around with us, is much more likely to be of benefit than if we try to tell them what to do. When minds are confused, and thoughts jumbled, having someone there with us, to listen and to try to understand, is likely to mean far more to us than if that person makes our decisions for us.

In a booklet produced by the Scottish Recovery Network,[39] users of mental health services talk of the importance of feeling in control of their experience. Two examples from this helpful booklet are included here:

> Initially I did feel very disempowered, that I had no control over my life . . . so I fell into things rather than actually making choices. If you're not actually actively making choices, you're not taking responsibility, and you walk into the victim's role (p. 19).

and

> They [mental health professionals] weren't saying, 'Well what do you think you need?' because I just didn't know. They were putting things in front of me and saying, 'We think this could be beneficial, what do you think?' and that made a big difference. They gave me a bit of choice. Realising that there were choices out there was a big step forward (p. 40).

Learning materials, produced by NHS Education in Scotland, in conjunction with the Scottish Recovery Network,[40] express it this way:

> If recovery is a journey then [our] role is to provide some guidance and signposts on that journey without taking control away from the service user [we] travel alongside (p. 21).

Awareness that, although training and expertise in treatment skills is, of course, essential for the provision of care, it is the *being there,* and *being myself,* that enables people in distress to find meaning and hope in their lives, is shared among many mental health workers. Nurses speak of the 'therapeutic relationship' and doctors recognise that the *relationships* they develop with their patients are crucial to the healing process.

---

39 Scottish Recovery Network, *Journeys of recovery: stories of hope and recovery from long term mental health problems,* Scottish Recovery Network, 2006.

40 NHS Education for Scotland and Scottish Recovery Network, *Realising recovery learning materials,* 2008.

Being there: as church

As Christians, committed to caring within our local community, the same is true: training and the use of appropriate pastoral skills needs to be balanced by relationships of partnership and of friendship. Caring is not about encouraging dependence. Our aim is to *be there* with people, in and through their struggles and difficulties. Committed to our local community, the aim of the pastoral care of the church is to enable people to discover, for themselves, the path that leads to well-being.

Being present – our *being there* with, and for, each other, is time-consuming and requires our commitment. But we are fortunate: the church has a history of commitment. In almost every town and village, there is a long-established Christian presence. Maintaining this presence is essential. By *being there,* and being committed to caring, we can enable our community to become a community of well-being.

Pastoral care – as defined in the chapter 'Swimming Pigeons' – is 'concerned with the well-being of individuals and of communities'.

In our pastoral care – our 'faith in action' – we work in partnership with others in our community, to ensure that justice flows like an everlasting stream, and that love of neighbour is shared throughout the community.

Pastoral care is about doing all we can to ensure that no-one in our community experiences rejection or prejudice *here and now*: it is also, however, about being committed to the search for justice for the future, and keeping hope alive, even though current policies may be unjustly enforced and oppression may be a present reality. 'Faith in action' is about keeping the hope of future justice alive, as well as working to make justice a reality today.

Pastoral care is about loving one another *just as we are*: it is also about loving each other into discovering our full potential and becoming who we are yet to be. 'Faith in action' is about keeping the hope alive that life will one day be experienced 'in all its fullness', as well as working to make well-being a reality today.

Commitment to 'faith in action' means commitment to *being there*: to being rooted within our community. The presence of the church – presence that is committed, faithful and ready to work in partnership with others – is a sign of God's presence and God's love. Our *being there* is a sign of hope: hope that well-being will be shared by all and communities of well-being created.

Being there and 'God talk'

It was Shabhana's need for the presence of another person there with her as she prayed that encouraged her to look out for someone who did 'God talk'. Her cultural background made it important that this person was female. Had this not been so, she may have chosen to pray with a fellow Muslim. But maybe not.

There are many reasons why people in distress may ask for help from someone they know is a Christian. The church has a history of being a caring organisation. People may feel confident that we will be able to help them, or that they can trust us. Christianity, of course, is not the only faith that is committed to caring for people in need. And people of faith are not the only ones able to show compassion. Nonetheless, we are people motivated by our faith to care, and many are aware of this. It is not surprising, therefore, that people turn to us for help.

Awareness that we are people who talk to, and who trust in, God, may be the reason that others come to us in their time of need. They may – or may not – want us to 'God talk' in their presence. But it is their sense that we have a relationship with God that makes them choose *us* to be alongside them and support them.

Living our lives, day by day, in such a way that people are able to see, and to sense, how significant our relationship with God is to us is, therefore, an important aspect of our *being there*. I hope that there was something in the way I related with the people in Shabhana's ward that led her to wonder if I was someone she could trust. I hope that, as she waited and watched, she saw in me something that gave her the confidence to ask Mohammed about me. I do not know if that was so: but I *do* know how essential it is that, in all we do and say, we somehow try to convey to those around us that we are people willing and ready to help, and people who can be trusted and relied upon.

'God talk' and prayer

When Shabhana took me into her dormitory to pray, I did not pray *for* her: she had her own relationship with God and prayed in the way she found helpful. In the sense that, in my own prayer, I asked God to help her, I did, of course, pray for her. But I did not assume – just because Shabhana had identified me as someone who was familiar with 'God talk' – that I had the right to pray *on her behalf.* Instead, I prayed *with* her. My intention, in doing so, was to help Shabhana sense our common humanity and our *shared need of God's help.*

There *are* times, of course, when it is appropriate to pray on behalf of another. When we ourselves are too ill to pray, or in so much distress that we find prayer impossible, we may appreciate the promise of a friend to pray on our behalf. When others are going through a time of depression or despair, they may be glad to hear our offer to pray for them. In my work as Chaplain, after spending time listening to a story of pain or distress, it sometimes felt appropriate for me to mention that, each evening at home, I always pray for people who would like me to. Many times, even those who I had spent time with, and who had told me they had no belief in God, asked – usually as I was preparing to leave – 'will you add me to your list tonight, please?'

Some of us may be unused to praying, especially if we have grown up in a tradition in which the minister, or the priest, is the only one heard praying aloud in worship. This can make it feel particularly difficult to ask for God's help for ourselves. People who have been taught that prayer requires specific words and phrases may feel inadequate, or unworthy. Being encouraged to 'tell God about your problem', or to 'say to God what you have just told me about how you are feeling', can help people to feel valued and to believe that God's love really *is* for them also.

Speaking of our faith is not essential for care to be 'pastoral'. Speaking of our faith is, though, an important dimension of our 'faith in action'.

Praying with others, likewise, is not essential to pastoral care. But it does have a place. It requires us to be sensitive to the issues and concerns of the person we are praying with, while remaining true to our Christian tradition.

'God talk' and pastoral care

The wording of the description of my job as a Mental Health Chaplain defined the role in this way: I was to 'offer pastoral care to patients, staff and carers of all faiths and none'.

Likewise, the pastoral care we offer, as Christians living in our local community, is for everyone; to people of all faiths and none. Whatever our beliefs, whatever our lifestyle, *everyone* has the need to feel loved, valued and accepted.

Our relationship with God – our own 'God talk' – is what directs the way we care. It is from God that we receive the strength and compassion, the challenge, the guidance and encouragement that we need, in order to care about, and to care for the people around us in ways that will enable their well-being.

The pro-active and re-active pastoral care that seeks to enable the well-being of all people is about making real the love of God in their lives. When justice flows through our communities and loving care is experienced by everyone, then the well-being of all can become reality.

Our aim is to transform the places we live into communities of well-being. God's Kingdom, we believe, will, one day, come to earth in all its fullness. That coming, however, is in God's hands, not ours. Until then, we do what we can, wherever we live on this earth, to share God's love as we love our neighbour.

With the help of God, and in partnership with the people around us, we do all we can to shine light into the darkness of injustice or illness, and to bring hope into lives worn down by stigma, depression or despair. Through this commitment to 'faith in action', we can enable one another to create communities of well-being from which no-one is excluded, and in which everyone is valued and accepted.

Chapter Ten

Conclusion

God created life to be good. We read in the book of Genesis that 'God was pleased with what he saw'. Land and sea, animals and plants, birds and trees, and human beings: *all* seen by God as 'good.'

This God who creates us is our Saviour God, who is with us, in our daily lives, encouraging us to live *well*. Throughout the pages of the Bible, we are reminded that living well means recognising our inter-dependence – our need for one another – as we live together in community. Living well means having respect for God, for one another, and for the whole of creation. Relationships rooted in respect are essential, if we are to care about, and to care for, each other in ways that enable the well-being of us all.

God created us to live *well,* and gives us a vision of what life can be like, when we work together to seek justice and love for all people. The world, God tells us, through the words of the prophets, should be and can become be a place where all live together in peaceful and caring communities. When swords are turned into ploughs, and spears into pruning-knives, there will be enough resources for everyone's needs to be met. When we 'do what is just', our communities can become places in which everyone is welcome, respected and valued. When we 'show constant love', we discover well-being, for ourselves and for others.

The vision God offers us is of the world restored as his 'Kingdom'. In his parables, Jesus tells us what this 'Kingdom of God' will be like. One picture Jesus gives is of God's 'Kingdom' as like a vast tree in which all the birds of the air can find shelter, build their nests and raise their young in safety. And this tree, we are reminded, began as a tiny seed.

Nurtured by God, as we journey in 'humble fellowship' with him, the seed of our faith is our motivation to care. Guided by God, we receive encouragement and inspiration. In the example of his life, Jesus shows us how to live, so that life in this 'Kingdom' might be experienced 'on earth, as it is in heaven'.

Guided by God, we discover how to care, and to ensure that our communities – like that tree in which all the birds of the air live peacefully together – are places in which *everyone* feels welcome, and accepted.

Enabling life to be lived *well* is the aim of our pastoral care – our 'faith in action'. It is as we create communities of well-being that we journey, together, towards the life in all its fullness that is God's promise for all the world.

* * * * * * * * *

This book has been written to encourage you to discover ways of enabling everyone in your local community to live *well*.

Throughout its pages, we have stressed the importance of respecting each other: of accepting one another *just as we are,* and of ensuring that *everyone* in our community feels valued and welcome.

We have looked at life as a journey, on which we enable and encourage each other – through whatever problems and difficulties – to live *well*.

Pastoral care – caring about, and caring for, each other – is our 'faith in action'. Our commitment to sharing God's justice and God's love motivates and guides us. In the stories and reflections, we have recognised the influence of this commitment to our actions. We have seen how our faith contributes to all that we do, in partnership with others, as we work *together* to create communities of well-being.

Your community needs God's justice. The people around you need God's love. *Your* community, then, needs *you*. The people around you need *your* church.

'Faith in action': the time to act is *now!*

Epilogue

I am here in Kanyakumari, at the southernmost tip of India. Yesterday a friend took me a few miles up the coast to ancient Vattakottai.

There, while being shown round the fort, I was delighted to discover familiar friends of mine: swallows swooping and diving around the ancient stones as they searched for insects to eat. These could be the very same birds that I had watched back at home, after they had made that amazingly long journey north to build their nests! Only two months ago, I had stood in a village, near seashore cliffs in the north of Scotland, watching as these incredible birds gathered – as they do in late summer every year – on the telephone wires. And then suddenly they were off; gone for another year, setting off on their long, arduous journey back south.

That day, as I stood on the cliff tops, I was dressed in coat, hat and scarf to keep out the cold wind that was blowing in off the sea. Nobody was paddling – as they are in their hundreds at this tip of India where three oceans meet. Here at the fort, a warm breeze is blowing and the sea is warm. Yet the swallows seem as at home as they were in the cold winds of home. The food they search for on the wing must be totally different here; the insects that live around here would not survive in the UK.

How adaptable these birds are: equally at home in these two so very different environments.

Today, as I walk through the market by the seashore in Kanyakumari, I notice a few of these beautiful tiny birds, perched on the wire just above the roof of one of the stalls. I pause, and look up, and a stall-holder comes over and looks upwards too. He seems puzzled. 'What you looking?' he asks me. I point. 'Oh, bird', he says, without much interest. I try to explain my excitement at seeing them – that these birds are familiar to me; that they come to my home country each summer. At my mention of 'home', my companion interrupts, kindly asking me 'which country coming?'

'Scotland', I reply. But after that, my lack of Tamil prevents further conversation.

Unrestricted by language problems, the swallows above us are adapting to their south Indian environment just as well as they cope with cool northern summers. Nature often seems so much more adaptable than we humans. Change is hard for us, yet life without change is impossible, and would become incredibly dull.

The journey of life has its 'ups and downs'. None of us can escape these, but together we can help each other through such experiences. We can support each other through hard times and celebrate together when times are good.

Alone, we struggle to survive: together, we are able to *live well*. With the help of God who is our Creator and our Saviour – we work together to create communities of well-being in which *all* find acceptance, hope and love.